DIVE SCOTLAND'S GREATEST WRECKS

DIVE

SCOTLAND'S

GREATEST

WRECKS

ROD MACDONALD

MAINSTREAM
PUBLISHING

EDINBURGH AND LONDON

First published in Great Britain in 1993 by
MAINSTREAM PUBLISHING COMPANY (EDINBURGH) LTD
7 Albany Street
Edinburgh EH1 3UG

ISBN 1 85158 532 X

A catalogue record for this book is available from the British Library

Typeset in Great Britain by Lasertext Ltd, Stretford, Manchester

Printed in Great Britain by Butler and Tanner Ltd, Frome

Front cover photograph: the Eagle Fleet tanker *San Calisto*, sister ship to
the *San Tiburcio*, sinking after hitting a mine (Courtesy Orion Publishing)

To my daughter, Nicola

CONTENTS

ACKNOWLEDGMENTS

This book would not have been possible without the help, encouragement and guidance freely and enthusiastically given by so many. Of necessity diving is not a solo sport. You have to depend on other divers and they in turn on you. In similar fashion it is impossible to carry out the underwater wreck surveys necessary for a book such as this without fellow divers and kindred spirits joining in to help.

My thanks must first of all go to my wife, Claire, who has been able to come along on most of the diving expeditions and help with the surveys. On other occasions she has seen me disappearing over the horizon, towing my boat to some distant wreck. She'll be dreading my next venture now that this epic has finally seen the light of the book shelves.

My heartfelt thanks must go to Ewan Rowell of Aberdeen, my regular diving partner who buddied me as we swam around Scotland's greatest wrecks, frantically trying to take in what we were seeing. Most of the underwater photographs are Ewan's work and I am grateful (if not relieved) to have got them. At one stage we thought that we were not going to get any underwater photos for the book at all as on dive trip after dive trip our cameras flooded, ruining the pictures. Ewan it seems is well known to most divers in Scotland! A former member of the Edinburgh University branch of the BSAC, and now with me in the Deeside branch in Aberdeen, Ewan has recently acquired Hollywood status after featuring in the dive videos, *Dive Scapa Flow* and the two *Dive Florida* videos. He is an extremely competent ex-commercial diver – for him the sea holds no fear. Those who know him will agree that his style is . . . to say the least, quite unusual. Those who don't know him can find Ewan's style sometimes alarming! Complete in his black rubber, ex-NATO Avon dry suit held together by patches and isoflex, along with his much-cherished 1960s twin-hose demand valve he makes a striking sight on any quay. Claire had her first dive with Ewan on the *Hispania*, in the Sound of Mull when we were surveying it for this book. We should have warned her what to expect – she has never been quite the same since! Ewan has been the most helpful and selfless buddy I could have had. We have had some tremendous dives and some great fun doing this book.

(We won't say anything about the endless hours we have spent steaming around in Aberdour Bay, magnetometer and echo-sounder beeping away, looking in vain for the long-lost bow section of the *Fram*.)

So many others have contributed in different ways. George Ritchie of Stonehaven, author of *The Real Price of Fish, Aberdeen Steam Trawler Losses 1887–1961*, was a fount of knowledge about the sea and was able to provide me with much information on the sinking of the *Fram* and *San Tiburcio*. Dave Tye of Oban Divers, perhaps the diver most closely associated with the wreck of the *Breda*, gave me a fascinating insight into his salvaging days in the 1960s when he and others spent several weeks digging out the *Breda*'s 8½-ton prop from its tomb of silt, blowing it off the wreck and lifting it to the surface. Captain Duncan McKelvie of the Puffin Dive Centre helped with much information on the present state of the *Breda*. The *Oban Times* gave me access to their old newspaper records which held fascinating accounts of the sinkings of the *Rondo* and *Hispania*. The staff of Stonehaven Public Library once again had to field requests for a never-ending list of obscure reference books from me. Many other sources gave me a wealth of information: the Imperial War Museum in London; Alex Macrae of Oban; the Hydrographic Department at the MoD in Taunton; the Maritime Information Centre of the National Maritime Museum in Greenwich, London; Lloyd's Register of Shipping; the U-boot Archiv in Cuxhaven, Germany; and the Royal Navy Submarine Museum in Gosport.

Ian Crawford and Peter Moir are the co-authors of *Clyde Shipwrecks*, the recognised guide to diving in the Clyde. Coming from the north-east of Scotland, the Clyde was not my home turf. Their book was an invaluable source of information and they both freely gave me much additional help and assistance with the wrecks of the *Akka* and *Wallachia*. I am much indebted to them for taking the time to give me and my fellow divers the guided tour of both ships, amongst others, and for their hospitality in putting us up and wining and dining us. They opened up the whole world of Clyde diving to me and I look forward to diving with them there again and reciprocating the courtesy up here in the north. Thanks too must go to Rab and Mary Morton of Kilmarnock for their kindness and the information they provided.

Rob Ward of Illusion Illustration Ltd in Bridge of Muchalls created the stunning paintings of the wrecks used in this book. As he did for my last book, *Dive Scapa Flow*, Rob, who is a non-diver and has never seen the wrecks, was able, with complete professionalism, to reconstruct what they look like today from original photographs, shipbuilders' diagrams and up-to-date photos and sketches that we could provide. His paintings bring the book alive and it has been a pleasure to deal with such a professional again. Once again, Ian Williamson of Aberdeen came to my rescue with his meticulous and much-praised cartography and outline drawings of the wrecks. Ian who, like me, has a great affinity with the sea, launched himself with great enthusiasm and ingenuity into this project.

His work brings perspective and realism to the wrecks. My secretary, Peggy Leslie in Stonehaven, bravely typed countless letters for me during the research for this book amidst the hustle and bustle of our normal business in a law firm. I would also like to thank George Brown of Inverness BSAC for the information he freely gave on the *San Tiburcio*.

I am indebted to each and every one of them. This book would not have been possible without their help.

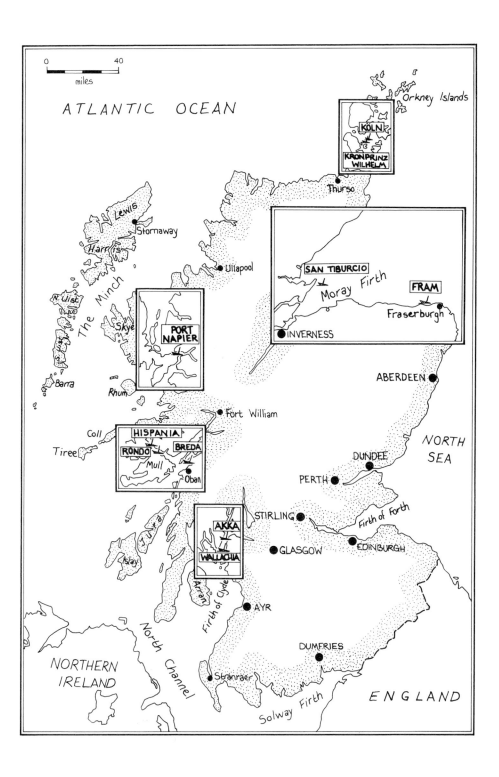

INTRODUCTION

Scotland's rugged coastline, its plunging cliffs and rocky outcrops provide literally endless dive sites, many of which are to this day unexplored. Through the centuries this same coastline has lured countless unfortunate vessels and mariners to their doom. Throughout history fierce winter storms have dashed helpless vessels on to rocks and sunk others without trace far out to sea. Reefs and rocky pinnacles rising menacingly from the seabed have snared the unwary, tearing open fragile hulls and consigning both ships and their unfortunate crews to the sea. Two world wars in this century alone have sent legions of vessels to their doom, easy prey for German bombers or U-boats. Scottish waters now conceal countless wrecks lying scattered all round their beautiful shores. A glance at any Admiralty chart reveals its own tragic story. Wreck symbols are dotted all around on nearly every chart. It is all too easy to forget that behind each and every simple wreck symbol there is a dramatic tale of an event that took many lives and altered or blighted the lives of all those who survived. Some sinkings are dramatic events of great heroism. Others are tales of great loss, suffering or personal tragedy. One thing is certain: for all of those souls who survived a wrecking the memory would be carried with them for the rest of their lives.

These wrecks were until recently only valuable for what could be salvaged from them and raised from the depths. Hard-hat divers, often using explosives to blast their way in, would strip many of the wrecks of valuable non-ferrous engine fitments, condensers and the like. On smaller wrecks this salvaging would result in almost total destruction of the wreck. The larger wrecks would suffer less from the salvor's attentions and survive relatively unscathed. Other wrecks would never be found by the salvors. Salvaged wrecks and lost wrecks, both would then over the years be forgotten, slowly passing from human memory and knowledge. The recent boom in scuba-diving has led to renewed research and interest in what lies beneath the waves around our shores. Sketchy details in old volumes of sinkings long ago have given vital clues which today's wreck hunter, with the benefit of electronic wreck-finding equipment, can use to 'rediscover' the lost wrecks. Sport divers diving for pleasure have accident-

Opposite: Scotland's greatest wrecks

13

ally discovered many lost wrecks around Scotland's shores. Local fishermen always know wreck sites as an area where fish congregate and where they tend to snag their nets. A few casual words from a skipper about an area of 'foul ground' has often led to divers investigating the obstruction and stumbling upon a lost wreck. Gradually the sea is revealing its secrets one by one.

The beautiful west coast and Western Isles of Scotland have always been a Mecca for divers. The rich sealife is fed and nurtured by the warm Gulf Stream waters that sweep the Atlantic coast. The picturesque Sound of Mull boasts many fine wrecks but two stand above the rest as being some of the greatest and most famous wrecks Scotland has to offer: the *Hispania* and the *Rondo*. The *Rondo* was driven from her anchor by a fierce gale and drifted with the strong winds and currents along the Sound. She drove on to a shallow reef running off the rocky islet of Dearg Sgeir in the middle of the Sound. Her momentum carried her onwards and she crashed and ground on to the rocks before coming to rest, perched precariously on top of the shallow reef. She lay there for several weeks before the storms finally drove her off and she slid off into the deep water at the side of the islet where she now stands almost vertically on her bows, leaning back against the near sheer underwater cliffs of the islet.

The Firth of Clyde has long been one of the busiest sea channels in the world and has seen a number of maritime disasters that have left an underwater legacy for today's scuba-divers to explore. In the days before radar the biggest threat to mariners was simply human error and the risk of colliding with another vessel. Fog lying on the river frequently limited visibility and created treacherous conditions. In 1895 the steamer *Wallachia* was passing down the Clyde on a voyage to Trinidad. Conditions were poor and a heavy fog descended. Suddenly, out of the fog appeared the bows of the Norwegian steamer *Flos* bearing down her. She was rammed and fatally wounded. She soon sunk and passed both from sight and from memory. The *Wallachia* was forgotten about and lay quietly on the bottom of the Clyde for 80 years until she was rediscovered in all her glory by local scuba-divers investigating a local fisherman's tale of an underwater obstruction.

The Clyde also boasts a number of treacherous rocks that have ensnared the unwary. The infamous Gantock rocks rise up from the depths to break the surface some way offshore from Dunoon. In 1956 they ripped open the hull of the large Swedish steamer *Akka* and sent her to the bottom. Her wreck, at 442 feet in length, is the largest in the Clyde and has now become a huge artificial reef supporting a rich and varied marine ecosystem.

Every diver knows about the treasure trove of wrecks that two world wars have left us at Scapa Flow in the Orkney Islands off northern Scotland. It is perhaps the greatest and certainly the most famous of all dive locations in the UK. In the cold depths of Scapa Flow lie the wrecks of the mighty German World War I High Seas Fleet. Three battleships and four light cruisers have lain silently in their watery graves since they were sent to the bottom on 21 June 1919 on the orders of the German commander, Admiral Ludwig von Reuter. The powerful Fleet, originally made up of 74 warships, had been interned by the Allies at Scapa Flow as a condition of the peace negotiations that would eventually lead to the Treaty of Versailles. Reuter, however, suspected that the peace negotiations, which had dragged on for seven long months, were about to break down and that hostilities would recommence. This would inevitably mean that the British would attempt to seize the Fleet and so he gave the order to scuttle, thus thwarting the feared British seizure. At Scapa Flow we have a unique underwater museum. Nowhere else in the world can divers drift over such a collection of fighting ships from the Great War. Although I covered these mighty wrecks in my first book *Dive Scapa Flow*, no book on Scotland's greatest wrecks would have been complete without including some of the Scapa wrecks. There are so many to choose from, each having something special, that it is unfair to pick only two as I have done. In the end I plumped for the light cruiser *Köln* and the battleship *Kronprinz Wilhelm*. They are two of my personal favourites and give a good contrast in styles between the sleek, fast, light cruiser *Köln* and the awesome scale of the mighty battleship *Kronprinz Wilhelm*.

Countless other vessels have come to grief at Scapa Flow over the years. Steamers have struck mines and trawlers have succumbed to fierce northern gales. The list of casualties at Scapa Flow is almost endless. The two world wars have seen their fair share of casualties, and many deliberate sinkings. 'Blockships' were scuttled by the Admiralty to block the minor sea channels into the Flow, thus preventing hostile vessels and particularly U-boats getting into the great natural harbour which was a major anchorage for the British Fleet. Some U-boats still attempted to break into the Flow but met their end doing so. One, however, successfully penetrated the British defences in 1939 and was able to attack and sink the British battleship HMS *Royal Oak* with the loss of 833 officers and men.

All down the east coast of Scotland there are scores of wrecks and I have chosen as examples the imposing wreck of the tanker *San Tiburcio* and the Swedish steamer *Fram*. The *San Tiburcio* sunk when she broke in two after striking a mine in the Moray Firth in 1940. The *Fram* was torpedoed whilst at anchor riding out a fierce storm. She too split into two sections, the stern drifting for 30 minutes before sinking.

On the stormy north-east coast there are many reminders of how cruel the gales that lash these exposed coasts can be. Dotted along the coasts there are many wreck sites known to local divers where unfortunate vessels have been driven on to the rocks. The heavy seas that pound these coasts in winter have resulted in these wrecks being dashed to pieces, the sites being little more than debris fields. The east coast is exposed to the full wrath of the sea, unlike the west coast where there are sheltered estuaries and channels between islands which protect a wreck and help keep it relatively intact. On the east coast of Scotland you need to go out into the deeper water offshore to find substantially intact wrecks.

The high quality of the scuba-diving, and particularly the wreck diving around Scotland is not as well known as it should be. If you're ever diving abroad ask your fellow divers what they would think about diving around Scotland. They will invariably feign a shiver and mutter something which loosely translates into English as: 'No way – it's far too cold and dark!'. Try explaining to them how good it is and see the look of disbelief spreading across their faces. Scottish diving obviously does not spring as readily to the lips as the Red Sea or Truk Lagoon! Those comparisons are, of course, unfair for such places are justly famous but Scotland still has much to offer the diver. Its rich and varied sealife and good underwater visibility, added to the wealth of wrecks make for great diving.

No longer is the cold the problem it was in the days of wet suits. Today's divers travel to the dive site in comfort in a warm, hard boat, often an old fishing boat, or are whisked to the dive site by a modern, fast Rigid Inflatable Boat (RIB) in no time at all. The wrecks are located by modern electronics, echo-sounders and satellite navigation systems. The dive is spent in warmth, cocooned inside a warm dry suit and thinsulate undersuit. Scottish waters have been opened up by these advances in diving technology. The RIBs have a greater range than the previous inflatables. More virgin dive sites are being dived and explored each year.

Literature about diving in Scotland is really still in its infancy compared to the more famous and exotic dive spots around the world. The boom in scuba-diving of the 1970s and 1980s has produced volume upon volume detailing the very best that these other locations have to offer. This literary outpouring has to some extent bypassed Scotland. Our rugged coastlines are far less heavily dived than in the south. There are countless miles of coastline almost completely undived. Who knows what secrets they will in time reveal?

Nowhere to date was there a book which easily pointed you in the direction of Scotland's greatest wrecks. If a visiting diver or non-diver wanted to ascertain which were the best he would have a difficult job. In the ten years or so that I have been diving I have had to rely on word of mouth about which were the great dives that Scotland had to offer and then go and try them for myself. Some lived up to the hype; others quite naturally turned out to be salty sea stories exaggerated as they were passed on.

The lack of good, hard information about the wrecks meant that a first dive on a wreck was always a voyage of exploration. How was the wreck sitting? Did it rest on its keel or lie on its side? Was it even upside-down? What condition would it be in: relatively intact or with its hull plates collapsing in? What would the visibility be like? Would there be strong currents whipping over the wreck? All these questions rush through a diver's mind as he prepares to dive for the first time on a new wreck. As he descends and leaves the safety of the surface far above, anxious eyes strain into the distance waiting for the image of the wreck to materialise out of the gloom. Inevitably what does appear bears no relationship at all to the image that the diver had formed in his own mind prior to the dive. I still look back with amusement at my first ever dive on the mighty battleship *Kronprinz Wilhelm* at Scapa Flow many years ago. No one ever mentioned to me before the dive the simple and important fact that she lay upside-down. The visibility was poor and I swam around for ages in the part of her hull at the bow that has been extensively salvaged, trying to work out just exactly what it was I was diving on. A little more information then would have made it a lot easier to understand what I was seeing.

The wreck of the *Rondo* in the Sound of Mull mentioned above is difficult to envisage unless you have dived on it or seen an illustration of how it lies. Her stern is only three metres beneath the surface yet the wreck plunges practically vertically down the sheer sides of a rocky islet to her bows resting on the seabed below in 50 metres of water.

This book then is designed to try and go some way towards filling the gap that exists in the literature. Inevitably it is a purely personal selection. These are the wrecks that I have found to be the most exhilarating. I have not included wrecks that are so remote that getting to them becomes a major undertaking. This book is intended to be a practical selection, a book that divers can readily turn to for instant, hard information on a particular wreck. The wrecks I have detailed can easily be reached by the usual combination of car and RIB. I have also not detailed any wreck which is a war grave. The wreck of the British battleship HMS *Royal Oak* torpedoed in 1939 at Scapa Flow is most certainly one of the greatest wrecks around Scotland. She is, however, a war grave and diving on her without the permission of the Admiralty is forbidden. There are many of the crew who survived the sinking and relatives of those who did not still alive today. Their feelings deserve to be respected.

No doubt I have missed out some wrecks that are up there with the best but it is purely a personal collection. On top of hard information on the wrecks themselves and the sometimes tragic circumstances of their sinking, I have tried to set out the other essential information that today's divers need. Boat launch sites, nearest compressor facilities and emergency centres are all listed for each wreck. I hope that you will have as much fun diving Scotland's greatest wrecks as I did. Behind each and every wreck is a story of great drama and human trauma. I am quite sure that each wreck would be worth its own individual book let alone the short story that I have pieced together. If you don't dive then I sincerely hope that you enjoy the book and the secrets of the deep that are now revealed.

Good diving,
Rod Macdonald

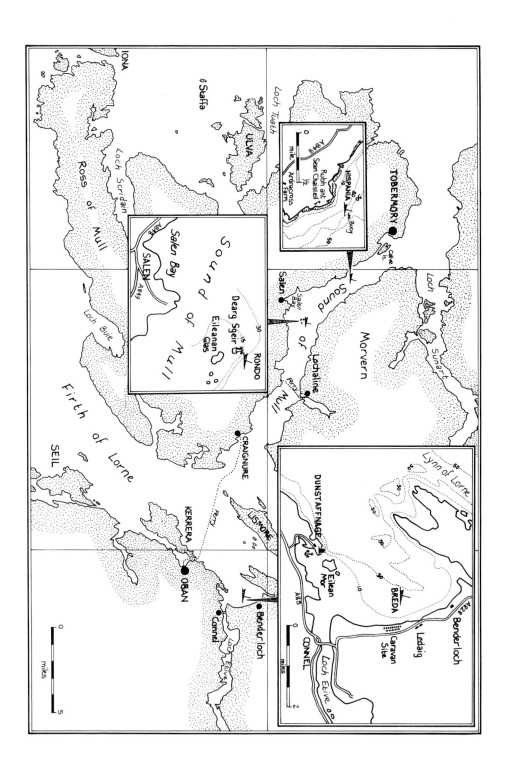

THE *HISPANIA*

Sound of Mull,
West Scotland

The *Hispania* was a steel, single-screw steamer built in 1912 by the Antwerp Engineering Company Ltd in Hoboken, Belgium on the River Schelde not far from Antwerp. The Schelde gave easy access for the newly constructed vessel to the Westerschelde Estuary which in turn opens into the North Sea near the south-east corner of England.

The *Hispania* measured 236.8 feet in length with a beam of 37.3 feet and a draught of 16.2 feet. She was built for Rederi A/B Svenska Lloyd and sailed under the Swedish flag after her registration in Gothenberg. Her gross tonnage was 1,337 tons, her net 644. She was powered by a triple-expansion steam engine and boilers developing 175 net horsepower (nhp), built by North-East Marine Engineering Company Ltd in Newcastle, the cylinder diameters being 20, 33 and 54 inches and the piston stroke 36 inches. She had a crew of 22.

The *Hispania* was designed with a main weather deck and a shelter deck below. She had five cavernous holds dropping down through two decks, three forward of the bridge and two astern. Her foremast rose up from the deck between the forward hold Nos 1 and 2. Her mainmast was located between the aftmost hold Nos 4 and 5. Both masts were fitted out with a derrick lifting system for loading cargoes into her holds. Two large derricks ran out from the mainmast over the top of hold No 4 to rest in their semi-circular mounts fixed at either side of the rear of the deck-house. At her bow was a distinctive raised companionway hatch facing astern. Heavy winches were anchored on the deck forward and aft of both holds Nos 1 and 2. Similar winches were located forward and aft of the mainmast between hold Nos 4 and 5.

The main superstructure which held the bridge, the engine-rooms and another large section of deck-house was located amidships between hold Nos 3 and 4. On the weather deck level the superstructure was ringed by a row of portholes. On the deck level above was the open bridge itself with, immediately behind it, the bridge deck-house itself studded with a row of portholes. Two large tubular steel ventilator funnels rose up from the weather deck at either side of the bridge. The bridge superstructure was a maze of interconnecting passageways and cabins dropping down

Opposite: Location chart of the wrecks of the *Hispania*, *Rondo* and *Breda*

through three deck levels to the shelter deck level. At either side of the bridge at main deck level was a covered walkway with a handrail inboard and railings to seaward. Portholes lined these walkways and at the end companionways steps led up to the higher deck level of the superstructure and to the bridge itself.

Immediately aft of the bridge were two further ventilator funnels and the single main funnel. Here also was the engine-room area with its distinctive fanlights and hatches at roof level. These opened upwards from the apex of its pitched roof to let fresh, cool air circulate down to the engines and crew below.

Aft of the pitched roof of the engine-room a large, square section of superstructure on two deck levels reared up from the main deck. Again this was lined with rows of portholes facing forward and doorways led into an intricate system of passageways, cabins and toilets.

Aft of hold No 5 and immediately in front of the stern deck-house was a small storage hold in which a spare ferrous propeller was kept for emergencies. The stern deck-house was much smaller in size than the two forward deck-houses, being raised only one level above the main deck instead of two. On top a handrail ran around it and at either side a lifeboat hung in its davit.

The rounded stern of the vessel was guarded by a handrail and dotted with mooring bollards. The rudder column rose up from the ship's keel to the main deck at this point and was connected to a large, T-shaped emergency steering windlass and quadrantle set in the middle of the deck. If the command system from the bridge was severed, chains could be attached to this windlass to allow direct manual turning of the rudder to port or starboard. Another hatchway set in the deck allowed access to the lower deck level.

The *Hispania* was a well designed, compact steamer which could carry a useful amount of cargo relatively inexpensively. She served her masters well for 32 long years at sea until disaster struck her on the night of 18 December 1954. She had arrived at Liverpool to load up with a mixed cargo of steel, asbestos, nylon fishing line and sheet rubber, bound for the port of Varberg near Gothenberg in Sweden. Once the laborious task of loading her had been completed she had cast off her mooring ropes on Friday 17 December and headed for the open sea on what was at first just one more routine voyage for this old lady of the seas. Her scheduled route took her out from the docks at Liverpool and across the Irish Sea, passing the Isle of Man. From there she had passed through the North Channel which separates Northern Ireland from south-west Scotland and then made her way out into the Atlantic. The *Hispania* steamed northwards up the west coast of Scotland, destined to round the north-west tip of Scotland before crossing the North Sea towards Sweden.

After leaving the Irish Sea her progress was painful and laborious as a fierce winter storm of driving wind, rain and sleet set upon her. Captain

ICB
OBAN 2078
1954

BILL
ssion

AND

SCOTLAND)
ment on
a second
mous on

plementa
ommission
poses the
mission of
c-organise
unties of
ire, Caith-
Shetland,
n of the
ll be situ-
es.

'croft" to
gs in the
gs in those
statutory

proposals in
v the com-
it is in the
community
he tenancy
ntee, how-
seal to the
absentee so
conditions,

the com-
ounce their
s under a
voluntary
the house
rating pur-
the croft

relating to
member of
vides for a
son outside
sent of the

loans to aid
ral produc-
at £200,000
assumption
of present
£100,000 a

cottars are
materially.
re expected
£10,000 a
ers for farm
5,000 a year
lly.

ovements
powers and
expected to
ny measures
t and social
arens. The

SWEDISH STEAMER SINKS IN SOUND OF MULL

Captain Goes Down With His Ship

THE Sound of Mull claimed another victim at the week-end when the Swedish ship *Hispania* went down in 14 fathoms of water after striking the Sgeir More, a reef about half a mile off the shore opposite Glenmorvern. Twenty-one members of the crew were saved, but the captain, 56-year-old Ivan Dahn whose home is at Gottenburg, true to the traditions of the merchant navies of the world, remained on board despite entreaties by the members of his crew, and went down with his ship.

The sinking took place on Saturday evening during a storm of wind, rain and sleet which made visibility in the Sound of Mull practically nil. The *Hispania*, which left Liverpool on Friday with a cargo of steel and was bound for Sweden, hugged the Scottish coastline to miss the worst of the storm and, after coming round the Ross of Mull turned into the Sound making for the open sea once again. She was nearing the westerly end of the Sound when she ran bow-on to the reef and stuck fast.

Alarming List to Port

After the engine was put full astern, with a shuddering motion the ship slid backwards off the rock but she was badly holed forward and had an alarming list to port. Despite the fact that she was making water quickly, there was no panic among the members of the crew who had time to get dressed and lower the two lifeboats and enter them.

All the members of the crew, except Captain Dahn, were in the boats and they rowed round the ship for almost an hour —the storm had abated by then and the water was fairly calm—and the members of the crew shouted to the Captain to leave the *Hispania* but he firmly refused.

"Suddenly the boat took a severe lurch —a bulkhead must have broken and the seas poured in—and without further warning she sank under the waves," a member of the crew said. "The last we saw of the captain was him standing in the deck house on the bridge, his hand up to his forehead in a salute."

With true Highland hospitality people from the Ardnamurchan coast cared for the shipwrecked sailors who landed on the coast at a point about half a mile from Glenmorvern Cottage about a mile and a half east of Drimnin. When in the boats the first officer, Walter Einarsson who is also from Gottenburg, noticed a dim light in the distance and after seeing what he decided were headlights of moving motor cars on the mainland, steered for that position.

Ashore at Glenmorvern

Only three-quarters of an hour's rowing took them to the shore and he and four others made their way up towards the light which proved to be coming from the window of the gardener's house at Glenmorvern, occupied by Mr Alistair Macdonald. They explained to Mr Macdonald what had happened and Mr Einarsson who speaks fluent English, said he wanted to telephone to someone in authority to report the sinking of the ship. Mr Alexander Macdonald, Achnasaul, who was in the house at the time and had his car outside, motored the first officer to the nearest telephone from which she police at Tobermory and Salen, Loch Sunart, were notified of the sinking.

Mr Macdonald returned to the house and he and David Lawrie of the Post Office, and Mr Logan from the Heritage, took the 21 men in their cars to Drimnin, the only spot the men could be lifted by the MacBrayne motor launch *Lochbuie*, which had been sent from Tobermory to take them off. At Drimnin the men were cold and shivering at the ship and Mrs Cameron, the local postmistress sent word down that she would make something hot for them. The men came up to her house in batches and they received a welcome cup of hot tea and something to eat. "It was a

There, Mr Andrew Noble, Lloyd's Agent in Mull, had made arrangements for the comfort of the men and they were taken to the Mishnish Hotel where they got a meal and then went to bed.

After a good rest the men went on board the *Lochbuie* at 11 a.m. to be conveyed to Oban where Bailie W. J. Calderwood, Western Area Manager for Messrs David MacBrayne Ltd., and local representative of the Shipwrecked Mariners' Society had made full arrangements for the comfort of the crew of the ship. The *Lochbuie* arrived at the Railway Pier at Oban shortly before 2 o'clock where Bailie Calderwood and Mr N. Hamilton Smith, Lloyd's Agent at Oban, met the officers and men and took them to the Royal Hotel where they were to stay until late afternoon on Monday.

Mr Duncan Kerr, the manager at at hotel, and Mrs Kerr, had had a busy time preparing for the men, for their chef was on his day off and they got down to the job of providing a four course lunch for the stranded seamen at short notice. The seamen had their meal as soon as they arrived in the hotel and afterwards they were interviewed by the customs officer and Mr R. Johnston Macdonald, Procurator Fiscal and members of the police force.

First Officer Einarsson, speaking of the sinking of the ship, said that he had been on the bridge with the Captain. "It was a bad night," he said, "and we were running into a blinding rain and sleet storm with practically no visibility.

"Suddenly we hit the reef with quite a bump and realising what had happened I gave the order to go astern. The ship came off easily but she took a 25 degree list to port and it was obvious that she had been holed and was taking in water.

No Panic Among Crew

"The crew were cries [on deck and they behaved splendidly and there was no panic. When it was found that there was no hope for the ship the lifeboats were lowered and the men were ordered to get into them. All of us left the ship with the exception of the captain who decided to remain on board."

The only Englishman on board, Francis Hattasley, a single man whose home is at Rippenden, Halifax, Yorkshire, told how the men shouted to their captain to leave the ship before it sank but he simply refused, although there was ample time and opportunity for him to do so. He was still on the bridge when the ship finally sank, he stated.

Two members of the crew have English wives, one living in Liverpool and the other at Salford, Manchester, and both had been with their wives and families only last week. They were anxious to get news of their safety to their wives on arriving in Oban.

Although most of the rescued men were fully clothed, some of the members of the crew who were on duty at the time the ship struck the reef, were still dressed in boiler

The dramatic events surrounding the sinking of the *Hispania* made headline news in the local press. The Oban Times, 25 December 1954

Ivan Dahn (57), who hailed from Gothenberg, held the *Hispania* close in, hugging the Scottish coastline to get some shelter from the worst of the storm. The following evening, Saturday 18 December, the *Hispania* rounded the Ross of Mull and turned into the Sound of Mull. The Sound of Mull is a narrow stretch of water some two or three miles across separating the Isle of Mull from mainland Scotland. It is about 15 miles long and at its northern end opens out into the Atlantic. It is no wonder therefore that the Sound of Mull is subject to fierce tidal surges as the awesome strength of the Atlantic tries to channel through this narrow passageway. Many treacherous rocks, reefs and shoals are dotted along the length of the Sound, making it a mariner's nightmare in bad weather.

By nine p.m. the *Hispania* was nearing the westerly end of the Sound, struggling against the storm in visibility which by now had been reduced to practically nil. The Sound of Mull is a particularly treacherous strip of water to be in in conditions such as this. The slightest deviation from course can spell disaster, as the many wrecks that lie here bear out. Unknowingly, the *Hispania* was off course and heading towards an unseen danger, the Sgeir More, a graveyard for many a mariner and vessel over the years. The Sgeir More, or Big Rock, rises up from the depths about half a mile offshore opposite Glenmorven. The *Hispania* drove on to Sgeir More bow on and stuck fast. Below decks the off-duty crew were pitched from their bunks by the impact.

Realising what had happened, First Officer Walter Einarsson immediately gave the order to go astern. The *Hispania* came off the reef easily but immediately started listing to port. She had been badly holed forward and within minutes she had taken on a 25-degree list to port. It was obvious to everyone onboard that her hull had been torn open by the reef and that she was taking in water fast. Her starboard anchor was run out to stop her drifting into greater danger in the treacherous tidal streams of the Sound. The crew were ordered on deck and dressed themselves quickly. Although she was shipping water rapidly there was no panic amongst the crew.

It was clear from the damage that there was no hope of saving the ship. The two lifeboats were lowered at the stern and the crew were ordered into them. All of the crew got aboard the lifeboats with the exception of Captain Dahn who elected to remain aboard his command. Members of the crew pleaded with him to leave the ship and board one of the lifeboats but he firmly refused. By this time the storm had passed over and the seas had become fairly calm. For almost an hour the crew rowed round the sinking vessel, shouting and pleading with the captain to leave his ship. He steadfastly refused even though there was ample time and opportunity for him to do so.

The *Hispania* settled steadily into the cold waters of the Sound and then suddenly gave a severe lurch as an internal bulkhead gave way under the weight of inrushing water. The remainder of her hull flooded quickly and without further warning she disappeared beneath the dark seas. Some survivors reported that Captain Dahn was last seen standing in the deck-house on the bridge as the ship went under, his hand up to his forehead in a salute. Others reported seeing him leaving the bridge and entering his cabin aft.

Once the *Hispania* and her captain had disappeared beneath the waves the crew in the lifeboats looked around for the nearest landfall. First Officer Einarsson spotted a dim light in the distance and then what he thought were the headlights of cars on the mainland. He steered the lifeboats in that direction as the crews rowed towards the distant shore. Three-quarters of an hour later they landed on the coast about half a mile from Glenmorven Cottage, half a mile east of Drimnin. Once ashore, First Officer Einarsson and four others made their way up towards the light whilst the others stayed with the lifeboats. The light proved to be coming from the gardener's house at Glenmorven occupied by Alistair Macdonald. First Officer Einarsson, who spoke fluent English, explained the tragic details of the sinking and asked where the nearest phone was to report the loss to the authorities. Once their plight became known the locals rallied round the beleaguered men and, in true Highland spirit, freely gave them every assistance they could. Alexander Macdonald of Achnasaul, who was also in the house at the time, had his car with him and drove the First Officer to the closest telephone from where the police at Tobermory, Loch Sunart and Salen were notified.

Alexander Macdonald then returned to the house and, along with other locals, David Lawrie from the Post Office and Mr Logan from the Heritage, drove the 21 men in their cars to Drimnin. This was the only spot where they could be picked up by the MacBrayne motor launch *Lochbuie* which had set out from Tobermory to pick up the crew as soon as their plight became known. At Drimnin the men waited patiently at the slip but, already wet, they were soon shivering, the cold winter air gnawing at their bones. With typical Highland hospitality the local postmistress, Mrs Cameron, sent word down to the men at the slip that she would have something hot made ready for them. The stranded crewmen came up to her house in batches where they got steaming hot cups of tea and something to eat. Speaking later of the incident she recalled: 'It was a job feeding 21 men without warning but fortunately, being so far away from the shops, we always have a good stock of food in hand so I managed quite well.'

Meanwhile the *Lochbuie* had arrived at the site of the sinking of the *Hispania*. When they set out from Tobermory the skipper had not known that the crew were safe and so had taken a large searchlight and breeches-buoy equipment with him. Whilst the *Hispania*'s crew were warming up and being fed by Mrs Cameron the skipper of the *Lochbuie* made a search around Sgeir More in the hope of finding the body of the captain but to no avail.

At about two a.m. on Sunday morning, fully five hours from the time when the *Hispania* hit Sgeir More, the men were ready to leave Drimnin.

The *Lochbuie* hove to as near to the tiny slip as it could and Mr MacLeod, the ferryman, assisted by Mrs Cameron's son, ferried the seamen out to the launch. After the short trip across the Sound to Tobermory the men were landed on the pier. Mr Andrew Noble, the Lloyd's Agent in Mull, had already made arrangements for the crew's comfort and the bedraggled men were taken to the Mishnish Hotel where they were given a hot meal and went to bed.

After a welcome night's rest the men went back on board the *Lochbuie* at 11 a.m. and set off for Oban, arriving at the Railway Pier shortly before two p.m. Once there they found that Bailie W.J. Calderwood, the Western Area Manager for Messrs David MacBrayne Ltd, the local representative of the Shipwrecked Mariners' Society and Mr N. Hamilton Smith, the Lloyd's Agent at Oban, had made further arrangements for their care. They were taken to the Royal Hotel where they were to stay until late Monday afternoon. Mr Duncan Kerr, the manager of the hotel, and his wife had a busy time preparing for the men as their chef was on his day off. At short notice they were able to put together a four-course meal for the stranded seamen. The men had their meal as soon as they arrived at the hotel and then they were interviewed by the Customs Officer, the Procurator Fiscal and the local police.

Although most of the rescued men were fully clothed, some of the crew who had been on duty when the ship hit the reef were still dressed in boilersuits and rubber boots. That Sunday night the Shipwrecked Mariners' Society made arrangements to get them suitably clad. Local shopkeepers opened up their shops to get the men supplied and the new, clean clothes were handed over to the men in the comfort of the Royal Hotel's lounge.

The crew remained in Oban until Monday afternoon when they caught the 4.45 p.m. train to London. On Tuesday they left the UK on a Swedish passenger ship bound for Gothenberg. A further search was made for the captain's body on the Tuesday but there was no trace of it. It was thought at that time that it was still in the deck-house.

The *Hispania*'s cargo of steel was salvaged during the 1950s. In 1957 a two-boat wire sweep was carried out on her by HMS *Dalrymple*. The sweep was clear at three fathoms and fouled at three fathoms and two feet. The wreck of the *Hispania* was then left to rest in her watery grave and forgotten about. In the 1960s a local clam diver, Dave Tye, came across her when he was asked to rescue a scallop dredge which had snagged on an underwater obstruction. He found it wrapped over the forgotten wreck of the *Hispania*. In the holds danger lurked for divers from her cargo of bobbins floating around suspended on invisible nylon monofilament line. If an unfortunate diver became snagged by the unseen nylon line then it could not be broken, only cut. In another hold were a number of brass propellers with a very coarse pitch, designed for lifeboats.

During the boom in scuba-diving of the 1970s the *Hispania* was

The stunning wreck
of the steamship
Hispania

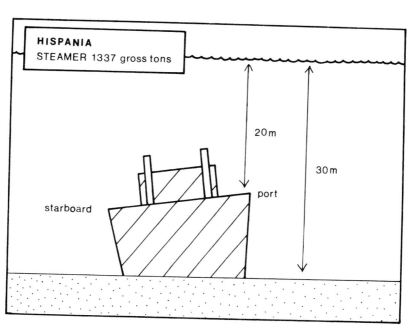

HISPANIA
STEAMER 1337 gross tons

20m

30m

starboard

port

rediscovered along with many other forgotten wrecks. The first detailed Admiralty records begin with a maritime survey in August 1973. It was reported then that her condition was good and she was sitting on her keel with a list of about 15 degrees to starboard. She was facing inshore to Mull, sitting on a rocky ledge, her stern overhanging it. It was noted then that her propeller had already been salvaged along with part of her cargo. The least depth over the top of her mainmast was three-and-a-half metres. Today her mast height has been further reduced to give a clearance over her of about ten metres.

The wreck of the *Hispania*, although now noticeably deteriorating, is still remarkably well preserved despite 40 years at the bottom of the Sound. She is perhaps the perfect wreck and is thought by many to be the greatest wreck in Scotland outside Scapa Flow: divers can usually be assured of good visibility over her; her holds, open superstructure, engine-room and deck fixtures provide endless sources of interest; and she has been covered by a particularly rich carpet of plumrose anemones and sea squirts, giving her a very distinctive orange and white colouring. She is now one of Scotland's most popular wrecks. At weekends and in the busy seasons of the diving calendar it is common to find several dive boats arriving over the wreck at slack water when the fierce tidal streams that flow through the Sound fade away. Divers can then explore the remarkable wreck of the *Hispania* and experience Scottish wreck diving at its best.

Today, the wreck of the *Hispania* lies in 25 to 30 metres of water in the middle of the northern section of the Sound of Mull at Latitude 56 34 57.0 N and Longitude 005 59 09.0 W. She is structurally intact and at 237 feet in length is small enough that her layout can easily be grasped in one dive. She has so much to offer that divers are drawn to her time after time, spending later dives exploring particular areas of interest to them. The classic combination of good visibility, a perfect wreck and great sealife make this one of Scotland's greatest wreck dives.

There are a variety of launch sites suitable for launching and retrieving a dive boat. If sea conditions are fair then it is possible to reach the wreck by sea from Oban, thus avoiding a long car journey to Morvern if you are coming from central Scotland. The journey is about 15 miles each way and on the best days in a RIB it will take in excess of an hour to get on-site, and, of course, the same back again. If the conditions worsen then it can be a very long, bumpy ride out and back. A spare petrol tank is mandatory on long journeys such as this. These are dangerous waters and no place to run out of petrol. The Sound of Mull has enough wrecks already – and they're a lot more interesting! After the morning's dive it is possible to have a pleasant lunch and refuel at Tobermory Bay at the north end of the Sound before coming back for the afternoon dive. Conveniently there is a petrol station right at the harbour entrance, only about 50 feet away from the steps where you tie up your dive boat.

Just a mile or two south of Oban on the narrow, unclassified coast road is Gallanach where there is a small harbour. Divers are welcomed here and there is ample parking for car and trailer and a reasonable slip into the water. At low water, however, the poorer part of the slip reveals itself and is quite bumpy and rough. There is a charge of a few pounds for launching and retrieving the dive boat. From here you can motor north up the sheltered waters of the Sound of Kerrera between the mainland and the nearby island of Kerrera, turning to pass through the channel at the northern end of Kerrera opposite Oban itself. From this point there is a five-mile journey across the Firth of Lorne until you pass between the famous Duart Castle, the Jacobite rebel stronghold of the MacLeans, and Lady's Rock with its lighthouse. Now in the Sound of Mull itself the dive boat flashes past the stunning scenery to Loch Linnhe, Scallastle Bay, the town of Lochaline on Morvern to the north-east and past Dearg Sgeir, a small rocky islet with a white lighthouse on it.

Dearg Sgeir is famous in diving circles as being the resting place of another great Scottish wreck, the *Rondo*, which stands on her bows leaning back against the underwater cliffs of the islet. Her bows are 50 metres beneath the surface, her stern only three metres. There is no other wreck in Scottish waters like the *Rondo*. A good way to see both wrecks is to dive the deeper *Rondo* in the morning, lunching at one of the pleasant harbour pubs at Tobermory Bay and then diving the *Hispania* at slack water in the afternoon.

Pressing on further up the Sound from Dearg Sgeir, a large, red channel marker buoy is visible from quite some distance, located in a direct line between Rubh' ant-Sean Chaisteal and Glenmorven Cottage. By RIB it is about 15 minutes from Dearg Sgeir and the wreck of the *Rondo*. This channel marker buoy doubles as a guide for dive boats looking for the wreck of the *Hispania*. Conveniently it lies only about 300 feet south-west of this buoy and is usually marked by a smaller buoy moored on to the bridge of the wreck.

The alternatives to this scenic but lengthy boat journey across the Firth and up the Sound from Oban are far shorter boat rides but from more remote and inaccessible launch sites – unless you are going to be staying at one of the dive centres. Lochaline Dive Centre on Morvern can be reached by road via the Corran Ferry and provides good accommodation, catering facilities, air fills and drying-rooms. There is a good slip at the harbour used by the vehicle ferry from which dive boats can be launched. Make sure that the ferry is not due in when you are launching your boat and clear the slip as soon as possible. There is a small jetty next to the slip and as soon as your boat has been launched get it away from the slip and over to this jetty. Dive boats can be tied up here and there are steps on it for getting gear down and loaded into the boats. From Lochaline it is about 30 minutes by RIB up the Sound to the wreck site. If you are staying on Mull itself for a week's diving then there are a number of places where a boat can be launched, such as Tobermory itself at the north end of the Sound. From Tobermory it is only a 15-minute RIB ride south to the site.

The Sound of Mull is extremely tidal with currents of two to three knots commonplace at mid tide. It is impossible to swim against currents that strong and so the *Hispania* should be dived at slack water to avoid any difficulties in staying on the wreck or getting picked up afterwards. Stories abound of divers, too scared to let go, clinging grimly on to handrails or other parts of the wreck whilst being swept horizontally by the force of the current. If you misjudge the tide you will spend your dive moving slowly from one handhold to another, fearful of letting go of the wreck for one moment and of being swept off downstream. Whilst surveying the *Hispania* for this book we managed to get the tides (which can be unpredictable!) completely wrong. The tide was starting to run as we went down on the wreck. When we poked our heads up from the shelter of the wreck at the end of the dive our masks were just about pulled off our faces with the force of the current. The mooring buoy was tied to the ventilator funnel at the port side of the bridge superstructure, about ten feet above us. We could see the mooring rope running off into the distance but there was no apparent way of reaching it. If we let go of the wreck and swam for it the current would have us halfway to Oban by the time we got up to the right depth. In the end we pulled our way round the base of the ventilator funnel until the current was on our backs, pressing us hard against the funnel. Then, with a leg wrapped round either side of the funnel, we shinned up it coconut-tree style until we

Near the very roof of the *Hispania*'s engine-room, a steel girder still carries the block and tackle which would have been used to lift heavy machinery below

could grab hold of the mooring rope and in due course arrive at the dive boat on the surface, our legs and bodies completely covered with a mixture of rust and decaying marine growth. It's easy to be wise after the event but don't let that happen to you – dive it at slack when the current will be negligible. Proper planning is essential to get the best out of the *Hispania*. A check of the local tide tables when planning the dive will pay dividends once out on the site. If you get it right you will have a memorable dive.

Normally a small buoy is moored to the wreck, usually on the bridge, and this provides a convenient point for RIBs to drop their divers. Larger hard boats will drop their divers a little upstream and let the current take them on to the buoy. It is best to keep hold of the shotline as you go down to ensure that what current there is doesn't drift you away from the wreck as you go down.

The underwater visibility in the Sound of Mull is renowned throughout the UK for its clarity. Twenty metres or more is a common report. On occasions visibility can close right in to five metres but doesn't really get much worse than that. Much depends on when in the year you are diving and the prevailing seas and weather.

The *Hispania* lies upright on her keel with a list of about 15 degrees to starboard which now seems to be getting progressively more pronounced. Her stern, in 30 metres, points into the middle of the Sound and her bows, in shallower water, point towards the shores of Mull. Although the depth to the seabed is 25 to 30 metres, most of the interesting areas – the bridge and the superstructure – are in the 18 to 25 metre range so a longish dive on her is quite possible. At her bow the port anchor is still in its hawspipe but the starboard anchor chain is run out to the seabed below. In the recent past divers have reported still being able to make out her name on the side of the hull. Nowadays, however, she has such a rich covering of sealife on her that her name is no longer visible. Right at the very bow itself, on the deck, is a raised companionway doorway facing aft with steps leading down below to the shelter deck. Aft of this is hold No 1 which appears to be smaller than the other four holds. The hatch cover would have been over the hold when she went down but this has now rotted away, leaving the structural ribs running across the hold exposed. Powerful steam-driven winches are fixed to the deck forward and aft of this hold. Two derricks have collapsed from the foremast (immediately aft of hold No 1) and lie over this hold running off towards the bow. The foremast with its A-frame supports rises up from the deck between holds Nos 1 and 2. Its cross-member is still in place but above that the mast has been broken off, possibly in one of the wire sweeps made by the Admiralty some time ago. Another set of winches sits behind the foremast and would have been used in combination with the derrick system to raise and lower cargo into the nearby holds.

Immediately aft of the foremast and between it and the bridge superstructure are two further open holds, Nos 2 and 3. These cavernous dark voids drop down through two deck levels. Handrails still line the sides of the deck, broken and rotted away in places. Aft of hold No 3 the square frontage of the bridge superstructure rises up for two deck levels. This is perhaps the most atmospheric and photogenic section of the wreck and worth spending some time exploring. Along the frontage of the bridge on the main deck level is a row of portholes, the brass and glass fitments themselves long gone. On the deck level above is the open bridge walkway and behind that the bridge deck-house itself, again lined with a row of portholes. It was in here that Captain Dahn was last seen, saluting as he went down with his ship. The roof of the bridge superstructure itself has rotted away leaving only the structural ribs. Standing on top of this superstructure you can look down and see the whole bridge open to view. It is quite safe to drop down into the superstructure to ferret around and meander through its maze of passageways and cabins. Looking down through three deck levels to the shelter deck level below, the captain's large, white enamel bath, now sadly cracked, can be seen towards the starboard side of the ship. The radio shack is also located here and still has its batteries in it. At either side of the superstructure stand the two large tubular ventilator funnels, the tops of which have been broken off, probably during the wire sweeps. The mooring buoy where you will start and end your dive is usually attached to the port side ventilator funnel.

At either side of the bridge superstructure is a covered companionway or walkway along which it is possible to swim. Inboard a single handrail is still fixed in position and to seaward the edge of the hull is lined with guard rails. A row of portholes allows a glimpse into the innards of the deckhouse. The walkway ends with a companionway staircase that leads up to the next deck level and the entrance to the bridge deck-house itself. At the rear of the superstructure, two companionway doors are open and lead inside.

Immediately aft of the bridge are the broken-off stubs of two small ventilator funnels, and, in between, the circular hole where the funnel once stood leading downwards to the engines below. The distinctive engine-room deck-house is located immediately aft of the bridge. In common with many ships of this era the engine-room had a pitched roof (as opposed to the flat roofs of the deck-houses) with hatches in it which could be opened to allow cool, fresh air to circulate. Some of the covers for these hatches are no longer in place and this allows easy entry into the engine-room for divers. At the very bottom the triple-expansion engine can be made out amidst the debris left from the salvagers' operations to remove the valuable non-ferrous engine-room fitments in the 1950s. Parts of the catwalks that gave the engineers access to the various valves and pieces of machinery are still in place and large pipes run off here and there at odd angles. Electric cables hang down from the roof, swaying in the gentle current. The most recognisable feature in the engine-room is a large piece of machinery with a distinctive circular crownhead valve at the front of it which still looks as though it would almost turn. On the wall nearby,

At the bow of the *Hispania* a raised companionway doorway faces aft towards hold No 1

beside an open doorway that leads out from the engine-room, is a switchbox, the fitments themselves long gone.

Immediately aft of the engine-room, a large, square deck-house super-structure on two levels towers above the main deck. Rows of portholes line each of its two deck levels. Like the main bridge, its roof, too, has rotted away, leaving its ribs and cross-members exposed. Looking up at it from the deck, the topmost row of portholes are filled with light streaming down from the surface whereas the lower row open into covered compartments and so appear dark. Sitting on top of this deck-house and looking downwards it is as though you are looking at a naval architect's layout plan. All the rooms and corridors are open and laid out before your eyes. It is possible to drop down into this superstructure, too, and wind your way through its maze of passageways to exit at the rear. The original wooden deck planking can still be easily made out.

Behind this deck-house can be found hold No 4 which is also open. The mainmast is situated between hold Nos 4 and 5 and two derricks are still fixed to it. One runs over hold No 4 forward to the deck-house where its furthest end rests unseated from its semi-circular mount nearby. Perhaps it was jolted from its mount as the ship went down. As with the forward holds there are twin, heavy, steam-driven winches forward and aft of the mainmast which would have powered the derrick system for loading and unloading the cargo. The mainmast has an A-frame on it with two smaller struts fixed to the deck and a cross-member. The mast itself has been broken off, leaving only about 5 metres of it now in place.

Aft of the mainmast is the last open hold, No 5. Behind it is a third deck-house, the stern accommodation, which is considerably smaller than the two forward deck-houses and is only made up of one superimposed deck level. Portholes line the deck-house and at the port side of the forward bulkhead an open doorway gives access and runs straight through with cabins leading off to exit at the rear of the deck-house. The remnants of handrails run around the top of this deck-house and a solitary lifeboat davit still stands in place, rising up towards the distant surface. Between this deck-house and hold No 5 there is a small storage hold in which sits a large ferrous propeller. This prop would have been kept as a spare in case of emergency and stored here to be as close as possible to the stern of the vessel in case the prop had to be changed. Two of its large blades protrude upwards out of the hold and bear the marks of many a diver's knife, inquisitive to see if the prop was ferrous or not. If it was non-ferrous it would have gone a long time ago.

Behind the aft accommodation the hull sweeps round to the stern. Handrails line the edge of the hull and set in the middle of the deck at the top of the rudder post is the emergency steering windlass, a four-foot-high, T-shaped column fixed to the deck. The gimbal and chains used to turn it can easily be made out lying on the deck at the base of the column. Mooring bollards with their ropes still wrapped round them are dotted here and there around the deck. Beneath the overhang of the stern the valuable non-ferrous propeller has been salvaged and removed.

The whole wreck is covered with a colourful profusion of plumrose anemones, soft corals and dead men's fingers, giving it an eerie, ghostlike feel. The *Hispania* was a relatively small vessel and can easily be circumnavigated in one dive. If a current is running it is possible to swim the entire length of the wreck inside it at shelter deck level, shielded from the tug of the current. There is abundant fish life with cod and saithe drifting over the wreck. Resident multi-coloured wrasse eye visiting divers inquisitively, perhaps hopeful of an easy meal from some prey disturbed by the divers' fin strokes. There is something for everyone on this wreck and so much to see and do that divers have to keep a careful eye on their watch. With so much of interest it would be easy to forget the rules and overstay the permitted bottom time. Because of the current normally found on this wreck it is advisable for divers diving from an RIB to head back to the bridge and ascend the mooring buoy line to the dive boat above. This will make doing a safety stop on the way up all the easier. As the divers ascend, the vivid, colourful lines of the *Hispania* blur beneath them and then, slowly, the wreck merges once more with the background. The divers are left in a void with neither the surface above nor the wreck below visible. You will always come up from the dive on the *Hispania* wanting to go back down on her again. Many divers do, time and time again. It is definitely a dive not to be missed.

Essential Information

Boat launch site: Oban. Gallanach pier. Lochaline pier, Morvern. Tobermory Harbour.

Tidal conditions: 2–3 knots maximum. Dive at slack.

Tidal constraints: Tobermory −0500 Dover, +0020 Oban. Salen −0455 Dover, +0025 Oban.

Visibility: 15 metres average.

Maximum depth: Seabed 30 metres. Deck 20 metres.

Coastguard: Oban (0631) 63720/9.

Police: Tobermory (0688) 2016. Craignure (068 02) 322.

Recompression chambers: Dunstaffanage Marine Laboratory, Oban (0631) 62244. Underwater Training Centre, Fort William (0397) 703786.

Air supplies: Oban Divers, Laggan, Glenshellach, Oban (0631) 62755. (Automatic coin-operated.) Lochaline Dive Centre (0967) 421662. (Automatic coin-operated.) Seafare, Portmore Place, Tobermory Pier (0688) 2277.

Hydrographic chart: No 2390, Sound of Mull.

Sea area: Malin.

Position: Lat 56 34 57.0 N, Long 05 59 09.0 W.

THE *RONDO*
Sound of Mull, West Scotland

The dry cargo ship *Rondo* had led a rich and varied life in several incarnations before she came to grief in the Sound of Mull in 1935. Her origins date back to the frantic days of World War I when the scavenging German Navy was taking a heavy toll on British shipping. By the start of the war the once great shipbuilding industries of the United States were only shadows of their past glories. The greater part of her shipping traded around North American coastal regions and the Great Lakes, sheltered from foreign competition by restrictive coastal reservation laws. In the great sea lanes of the Atlantic and Pacific only a few liners and cargo carriers carried the Stars and Stripes. The American shipbuilding industry was truly in its final death throes. In 1914 a mere 175,000 tons of new US shipping was launched. By the following year it had dropped to 150,000 tons. However, the Great War, so destructive for Europe's trade and industry, would save the US shipbuilding industry from oblivion.

In Europe, the British Government realised that the hard-pressed British shipyards could not turn out enough new ships to replace those lost by German naval action. By the end of 1915 some 1,600,000 tons of British shipping had been sent to the bottom. The effects of this were also felt in other countries such as Norway and the Scandinavian states which had previously had much of their shipping built in Britain.

Far removed from the destruction of the war, the potential of the failing American shipbuilding industry, with its unending steel supplies, to assist the Allied effort was realised. Even American shippers who had previously turned to the British and foreign yards for their new ships now found that they had to look closer to home to find shipbuilders able to build the ships that they needed to carry their cargoes. Once all British and foreign competition had effectively been removed from the scene, the US, which at that stage was not in the war, removed their coastal reservation laws and actively encouraged the transfer of foreign ships to the US flag for safety.

The flood of new shipbuilding orders from abroad was so great that old, ailing yards suddenly had to be enlarged and updated. Scores of new yards were opened up, bringing added benefits to the local communities from the secondary industries they fostered. By March 1917 new shipping contracts for the Red Ensign amounting to nearly three-quarters of a million tons had been placed. Contrast this with the figure for 1915 of 150,000 tons and you get some idea of the scale of the surge in shipping orders for the American yards.

All these new vessels were to be constructed to standard designs, standard hull types and engines. These 'standard ships', excluding the later concrete ships, were all given a standard nomenclature with the word *War* being prefixed to their names.

On 6 April 1917 America declared war on Germany and entered the fray. On 17 April the Emergency Fleet Corporation was formed and, in turn, called for the setting up of the United States Shipping Board. The Board studied the existing shipbuilding situation in the US in the light of the new military needs which now had absolute priority. Their review made clear that, except where prior reservations had been made by the US Government for the construction of naval vessels, all the other US yard capacity was already full with orders for merchant ships for American and foreign owners. They concluded that there was no possibility that the existing yards would be able to provide the necessary new ships for the US war effort as things stood. Something drastic would have to be done to alleviate the situation.

The Board therefore requisitioned all merchant vessels which were then under construction in US yards, be they on the stocks or at fitting-out-berth. The effective date of the requisition was 3 August 1917 when some 400 hulls were swiftly transferred into US Government ownership. At this time the *Rondo* was under construction ostensibly for the Cunard Steam-Ship Company but in reality for the British Government. At that stage she was known as *War Wonder (I)*. (When the orders for all these new ships had been originally placed America was not in the war and accordingly had a neutral status. The new orders therefore had to be placed through an agency and not directly by the British Government as a way of getting around America's neutrality. The Cunard Steam-Ship Company was used by the British Government to get round this technicality.)

Once the American requisition had been made nearly all the original names for the vessels were abandoned overnight. Of all the orders placed with American yards, only a total of eleven steel and two wooden vessels were completed and delivered to Britain. One vessel at least, the *War Fox*, sailed under the American flag under her *War* name for a short while. Another vessel, the *War Sword*, was actually completed and despite being requisitioned was released to the British in September 1917. Only a few survived with their original names. Once requisitioned by the US the *War Wonder (I)* was promptly renamed the *Lithopolis* and was completed in September 1918, only two months before the Armistice halted the fighting.

The *War Wonder (I)* was one of the 3,500 tons dead-weight tonnage (dwt), standard dry cargo ship class. She had a gross tonnage of 2,363 and was built by the Tampa Shipbuilding & Dry Dock Co in Tampa, Florida. She measured 264 feet in length with a beam of 42 feet. Her moulded depth was 24 feet two inches and she had a draught of 21 feet two inches. She was powered by triple-expansion engines constructed by her builders, developing 1,200 indicated horsepower (ihp). She, like all the standard ships, was a slow vessel with a cruising speed of only ten-and-a-half knots.

With the Armistice of November 1918 halting hostilities, most of the new British ships then on the stocks and at fitting-out-berths became redundant and were sold off to commercial interests. They would then be adapted and completed to the new owner's individual specifications. This accounts for the frequent variation in the build of these 'standard ships'.

In all some 3,500 such tramp ships were built and after the war the Board had a real problem about what to do with this mass of surplus shipping. Many ships were broken up. Some were laid up in rivers and backwaters until they found use again in World War II. Others were sold for whatever could be got for them. One huge batch of 200 tramp ships was purchased by the Ford Motor Company for scrapping in Detroit and eventually ended up on America's freeways as automobiles. The *Lithopolis* was renamed *Laurie* in 1930 and then finally in 1934, the *Rondo*. This was a name that would not live long with her. It was a name that she would take to her grave.

As 1934 turned into 1935 the Depression bit hard at Britain's economy and industry. During the last days of January 1935 the recently renamed *Rondo* set off in ballast from her berth in Glasgow's docks on the Clyde. She passed out into the Firth of Clyde and then into the North Channel of the Irish Sea. Her route was scheduled to take her round the north of Scotland and then down the east coast, passing the Farne Islands, to Dunstan in Northumberland on the north-east coast of England. At Dunstan she would collect her cargo and head off on her scheduled journey to Oslo. On the journey north, on 25 January, the *Rondo* was forced to halt her journey in Aros Bay, near Tobermory in the Sound of Mull to take shelter from a raging blizzard.

Mountainous seas crashed against the side of her hull, driving sheets of spray over her deck and superstructure. White crests of foam flew off the waves and were carried quickly away by the high winds. The *Rondo* shuddered as she lurched with the impact of each wave, her anchor chains straining to hold her in position. The crew soon became accustomed to the regular movements of the vessel as the early evening darkness swallowed the *Rondo* and her surroundings merged into blackness. Her crew braced themselves to pass an uncomfortable night, riding out the storm.

After a few hours, just after nine p.m., the now familiar rolling pattern of the vessel changed markedly. Instead of the lurching fight against the seas, the *Rondo* started to wallow freely. A furious blast had wrenched her from her moorings. She was now drifting powerless in the Sound in an easterly direction towards Salen, being driven on by the wind and tide.

Her crew stared anxiously out into the driving seas, watching the path she was taking along the Sound. Their eyes stung with the sharp bite of the seawater being blasted against their faces. For ten long miles their luck held out as the *Rondo* drifted helplessly in the pitch darkness. Suddenly out of the gloom the small, rocky islet of Dearg Sgeir, near Eileanan Glasa (Green Island), with its distinctive white lighthouse, reared up ahead directly in front of the ship. Her rocks were a mass of breaking surf as furious waves pounded on to them, exploding in the darkness in an iridescent display.

The *Rondo* perched high on a reef at Dearg Sgeir soon after being stranded. She is still making smoke and one of her lifeboats has been partially lowered from its davit in the confusion of the stranding (Private Collection)

It was too late successfully to take any evasive action and the *Rondo* crashed on to the north-west side of the 100-foot-wide islet. The momentum of her 2,363 tons following on behind drove her up on to a shallow, submerged, rocky reef close to the lighthouse itself. The air was rent with the sickening sound of her steel hull crashing and grinding on to the rocks. The momentum of the *Rondo* carried her some way on to the reef until she came to a halt, with all 264 feet of her balanced precariously on the reef, practically high and dry. Mercifully none of the crew had been injured and they were able to peer over the sides of the ship and take stock of their surroundings from an unusual viewpoint for a seaman. At least they were in no immediate danger.

The crew set off distress signals and these were seen from the shore. An SOS was immediately sent to Tobermory and two Fleetwood trawlers, the *Norina* and *Daily Herald* FD 101, set off to assist the vessel in distress. The first radio report of the disaster was picked up at the Malin Head wireless station which received a brief message from the British steamer *Lochmor* at 10.30 p.m.: 'Norwegian steamer *Rondo* grounded Eileanan Glasa, Salen, Sound of Mull; requires assistance.' At 11.45 p.m. another message was picked up, this time from the *Rondo* itself: 'Want tug as quickly as possible; crew still onboard, temporarily safe.' At 2.28 a.m. a further message was received: 'Standing on rock; leakage in both holds, temporarily saved.'

The cold, grey dawn of 26 January revealed the full plight of the *Rondo*. Holed forward, aft and amidships she lay practically on an even keel with only a slight list to port, broadside on to and dwarfing the small rocky islet. The two Fleetwood trawlers *Daily Herald* and the *Norina* got towing lines aboard the *Rondo* and made several unsuccessful attempts to tow her off the reef. They were joined later by the *Electra II*, H 661 and the fishery cruiser *Minna* and collectively they made further attempts to drag the *Rondo* off the rocks. Despite the combined efforts of all four vessels the *Rondo* could not be budged and the trawlers were getting damaged in their vain attempts. The *Norina* damaged her bulwarks and the *Daily Herald* and *Electra II* fouled their propellers with wire warps. The attempt was abandoned and the two disabled trawlers had to limp back to Oban, convoyed by the *Norina*, for repair, leaving the fishery cruiser *Minna* standing by to take the crew off if an emergency developed. They had all remained aboard and it was considered that they were quite safe meantime.

The trawlers arrived at Oban at two p.m. on Saturday 27 January and had to engage a diver and an engineer to work over the weekend to clear the wire warps from their fouled propellers and repair a warped propeller.

If the *Rondo* was to be saved she would have to be pulled off the rocks and it was obvious from the failed attempts that more pulling power was needed. A tug was sent for and another attempt was set up for Monday. The Greenock tug *Chieftain* arrived on site on time but after surveying the *Rondo*'s plight judged it inadvisable to attempt to refloat her until a thorough survey had been carried out by a diver and any necessary repairs attended to. Any movement of the ship might mean her sinking in deep water.

By the following day (28 January) the first salvage experts from a Liverpool salvage company had arrived on the scene and, after an initial inspection, judged that for any attempt to refloat her to be successful the operation would have to be delayed until suitable high tides in the middle of the following week, about ten days away. This attempt, like the others, failed and when another salvage vessel from Sunderland, the *Reclaimer*, arrived on the scene a week later, on 5 February, the *Rondo* was still high and dry defying all efforts to save her. After surveying the vessel at high tide it was finally decided that she could not be saved and she was given up as a total loss. The crew had remained aboard for the fortnight since

she ran aground, keeping her boilers fired to give them warmth and power. They were now taken off the stricken vessel and the *Rondo* was abandoned to await her fate.

Eight of the crew started out for their homes in Norway on 4 February. The remaining 14 arrived with all their belongings at Oban on the motor vessel *Lochinver* on 7 February *en route* for Norway. The *Reclaimer* started the return journey to Sunderland on the same day and the master of the *Rondo* remained on Mull for the time being. The *Rondo*, it had been decided, would be broken up where she lay.

A salvage crew quickly appeared on the scene and over a period of several weeks systematically stripped the vessel, removing large sections of her hull and cutting most of her right down to below her old waterline. The effects of the harsh winter weather in the Sound began to take effect and the *Rondo* started to creak and groan as she was battered by seas washing over the islet, rocking slowly back and forth. Inch by inch, almost imperceptibly over the weeks, she was pushed further over the rocky reef.

The *Rondo*, aground on Dearg Sgeir some time after being stranded but before salvage operations had commenced. The angle of her incline has increased since the earlier photograph was taken. Her propeller, formerly half submerged, has lifted completely above the water and her bows have moved into deeper water (Private Collection)

The salvage crew who had been living aboard whilst they stripped her, fearing for their own safety, moved off and set up camp on the small patch of ground beside the vessel, working aboard her by day and camping there at night.

According to local legend two would-be salvors from Fife now came into the picture, setting up a base on the mainland shore. The story goes that each night they would row across from their base some two miles distant. Whilst the official salvage gang slept the two would scour the wreck for valuable non-ferrous metal. They would rely on the groans and creaks of the tortured vessel to disguise their own sounds as they removed as much as they could carry before rowing back to their base. How much truth there is in that story is not clear but it is the stuff that legends are made of.

Gradually the fierce tides and storms in the Sound pushed the *Rondo* over the reef. Her decks began to slope down forward as her bow dipped into the deeper water beyond the reef. Her stern lifted clear of the water, exposing her propeller which had initially been half submerged. The angle of her incline increased as time passed and it became clear that it was only a matter of time before she went right over and plunged bow first into the depths below. The salvors, knowing full well what was going to happen, raced against the clock to get as much of her as they could before her final journey into the depths.

Eventually the irresistible ravages of the sea pushed the *Rondo* from her precarious pedestal. She slipped slowly off the far side of the reef, bow first. Once her centre of gravity had shifted her tilt became more

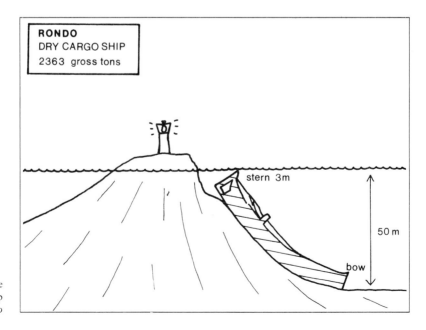

The wreck of the dry cargo ship *Rondo*

pronounced, her plating grinding on the rock beneath her. Once on the move she gathered momentum and forged her way down into the water. Once capable of floating, she was now a broken ship, her dead weight dragging her down the side of the reef. The dark seawater boiled and frothed as she plunged down the sheer underwater cliffs of the islet. The rocky sides of Dearg Sgeir plunge nearly vertically at first for approximately 30 metres and then begin to level out to a flat bottom at 50 metres. The bows of the *Rondo* plunged down these underwater cliffs towards the seabed 50 metres below. As she struck the soft bed she ploughed into it, bottoming out her descent until she slowed to a stop. Vast clouds of silt were sent billowing up from the seabed. She came to rest practically standing on her bows and leaning back against the sheer rocky side of the islet. The tip of her distinctive rudder post stopped just beneath the surface at three metres, her bows far beneath in 50 metres of water. She is a most remarkable wreck. There is none other like her in the UK.

Today the *Rondo* lies in the same position as when she slipped off the reef in 1935; hard against the north-west side of Dearg Sgeir in the middle of the Sound of Mull, north-east of Salen Bay at Latitude 56 32 16.5 N and Longitude 05 54 40.0 W. She lies immediately to the east of the small lighthouse on the rock and a small buoy is often attached to her uppermost stern, only about 70 feet from the rocky islet itself.

The *Rondo* lies about five miles south of the *Hispania* in the Sound of Mull and it is perfectly possible to dive both wrecks in one day, diving the deeper *Rondo* first. The access to the site is exactly the same as for the *Hispania*. A lengthy RIB ride of about one hour from Oban, across the Firth of Lorne, will see you on site above the wreck. A hard boat will take far longer to get there and is not really feasible for a day trip. Alternatively there are shorter boat trips from Finunary and Lochaline on Morvern and Salen and Tobermory on Mull itself.

Like the *Hispania* the *Rondo* is best dived at slack water to avoid any complications with the tidal pull through the Sound. The currents here are up to about 0.7 knots, not nearly as strong as on the *Hispania* where the current can easily reach two to three knots, but still more than enough to make your dive uncomfortable. If you don't dive her at slack you will have to cling to the buoy line as you go down. Once on the wreck you will have to make sure you are holding on to a convenient part of it at all times. The force of the current will keep you alert and looking for handholds. I saw one diver who missed a handhold swept off the wreck as though he were a piece of cork to surface a minute or two later about 150 feet downstream of the dive boat.

Anchoring above the wreck itself it is difficult to visualise what lies beneath. Wrecks normally lie on their keels, sides or upside-down. They just don't come standing upright on their bow! As the divers drop into the water at the start of the dive and congregate at the buoy they can vaguely make out the outline of the distinctive rudder post beneath them.

Opposite: The dramatic wreck of the dry cargo ship *Rondo*

If they have hit slack water properly there will be no current to worry about on the wreck.

The divers start to descend down the buoy line which is tied to the rudderpost and soon the outline of the stern materialises from the darkness below. The uppermost parts are covered in waving strands of kelp. As they reach the wreck itself they descend towards the bottom of the rudder. The propeller is long gone – it was one of the first things to be removed during the salvage operations in 1935. The brass bearings at the end of the prop shaft, however, are still clearly visible. At about 10 metres this is a good point for divers to collect their thoughts and ensure that their diving partner, or 'buddy', is alright and ready to press deeper. Looking from the wreck towards the seabed at either side of the wreck, the divers

Dearg Sgeir and its distinctive lighthouse seen from above the wreck of the *Rondo* with the island of Mull in the background

see the flat plateau of the reef top immediately below. The reef ends abruptly at a drop-off as the smooth rockface of the cliffs plunges almost vertically down into an inky darkness below. It becomes clear that the remains of the *Rondo* actually sit in an underwater chasm or small gulley which snugly accommodates her and runs vertically down towards the seabed. This explains why the *Rondo* has remained standing upright on her bow all these years. Had she not been wedged in this gulley she would surely have been swept over on to her side by the force of the current that forges past her. The near vertical cliffs at either side of her are so smooth that it is almost impossible to stand on them and keep your footing.

The Sound of Mull is rich in sealife and all around the divers, wrasse, cod and saithe drift by, eyeing them and watching carefully to see if the divers' fin strokes dislodge or uncover any food for them. The plates of the hull are covered in a rich and colourful profusion of dead men's fingers, plumrose anemones and sea squirts. Once a home for man, the wreck of the *Rondo* has become home for countless marine creatures who find shelter and food in its intricate nooks and crannies.

Looking down below, the divers can see about 10 to 15 metres down the wreck itself. It seems to plunge into a black, bottomless pit well beyond the limit of their visibility. For some people this feeling of floating above a black void can be quite disconcerting. The bottom is far below, well out of sight.

Once ready, the divers start to descend down the wreck. Soon the kelp which clings to the shallowest parts of the structure thins out and then disappears to reveal the bare lines of the wreck itself. The extent of the progress the salvors made in cutting her down for scrap is soon apparent. As the divers move downwards from the rudder to the stern of the vessel they can see both sides of the hull sweeping back up towards them to meet at the rudder. Inside the confines of the hull it is quite open as all the superstructure and decking is gone. The hull has been cut right down and gutted to expose the ship's ribs and the prop shaft which rises up to exit at the rudder.

Further below, at about 15 metres, a large square section of the starboard side of the hull (which would originally have reached up to the main deck) has been bent over almost at right angles to lie across the centre of the wreck. This section runs for about five metres across the starboard side of the wreck and drops down for about eight metres. It looks as though the salvors had cut away hull plating around this section and made it ready to be removed too. Perhaps the final plunge of the *Rondo* prevented them from removing it and it was bent over the wreck in her tumultuous final descent. The port side of the hull here also looks as though it has caved in on top of the innards of the wreck.

As the divers continue the descent they feel the increasing water pressure on their ears. The discomfort is eased by 'popping' the ears in much the same way as in a plane. The increasing water pressure compresses the

neoprene of the divers' warm dry suits, reducing their buoyancy, with the effect that they become heavier in the water and start to sink faster. The divers adjust their buoyancy as they descend to maintain a delicate equilibrium of neutral buoyancy. Here a diver is perfectly balanced in the water, neither sinking nor floating to the surface. Neutral buoyancy is achieved and maintained by bleeding air from the air tank on his back into the dry suit or alternatively into a buoyancy compensator as he descends. This process has to be repeated several times as the diver descends due to the progressively greater compression of the dry suit and corresponding loss of buoyancy. (Similarly, when a diver ascends the compressed neoprene of his dry suit expands and regains its former thickness. This increases his buoyancy, making him positively buoyant and a diver must vent off air from his suit or buoyancy compensator to regain neutral buoyancy.)

At about 25 metres down, the goalpost A-frame base of the mainmast looms up out of the gloom, the most recognisable feature on the wreck. The mainmast itself has been removed just above the cross-member of the A-frame support. Just aft of it and now above it, a deck winch still stands on an intact section of the main deck and a small derrick arm points upwards towards the distant surface. Further aft and now above the winch, part of the rim of a hold can be made out although the main deck ends abruptly where it has been cut down by the salvors. The mainmast itself has broken and fallen down to lie vertically, almost along

A sturdy steam winch lies immediately above the *Rondo*'s mainmast A-frame on the near vertical deck at about 25 metres

the centreline of the wreck and pointing straight below into the depths. In the gulley on the starboard side of the wreck lies a derrick and much scattered wreckage. On the port side a large hole in the hull plating allows divers to pass through it and grasp the scale of the wreck from outside. Looking up from underneath, the A-frame mast support can be seen rising up through the shelter deck and then the main deck, silhouetted against the distant surface.

As the divers pass further down they drift over the area where the bridge superstructure and engine-rooms would once have been. This area has been heavily salvaged and cut down and now there is only a mass of broken spars, collapsed plating and scattered ship's fixtures. As they descend, the natural light filtering down from the surface fades and the surroundings become dark and gloomy. Beneath them the wreck plunges straight down into the darkness, the bottom still well out of sight.

At a depth of 38 metres the divers pass beyond the main wreckage area into the bow section and what would have been the forward holds. The wreck has started to bottom out over the last ten metres and it no longer plunges straight down as before but seems to shelve or flatten off. Here the innards of the wreck are filled with silt with no real features of note. The sides of the hull, although still extensively cut down, are intact with the structural ribs easily visible. Gradually the sides of the hull sweep together towards the bow which rests in just over 50 metres of water, which is the recommended maximum depth for sport divers. All too soon at this depth the divers' permitted stay or 'bottom time' is reached and it is time to retrace their steps up the wreck towering above to the distant surface. Because of the depth the divers will be very careful not to surface too quickly to allow the large quantities of nitrogen absorbed into their bloodstreams to leave their bodies harmlessly and avoid any possibility of decompression sickness, commonly known as the bends.

It is important at this depth to remember that each diver will be suffering to a greater or lesser degree from nitrogen narcosis, commonly called the narcs and christened by Jacques Cousteau as the 'raptures of the depths'. As the water pressure surrounding the diver increases with the increasing depth it is essential that the air in the diver's lung cavities is at the same pressure to maintain an equilibrium or balance between the water pressure outwith the body and the air pressure in the lungs. If this delicate balance is maintained then the diver will come to no harm. If the lung pressure were to fall below the water pressure pressing on the diver's body then his lungs would be crushed by the greater water pressure. At 40 metres the water pressure is five times the atmospheric pressure that we all breathe air at on the surface. The net effect is that at 40 metres the diver has to take into his lungs five times the amount of air that he would on the surface, simply to fill his lungs in the normal way. The diver's aqualung or regulator automatically delivers the correct amount of air to maintain his equilibrium.

Air is made up of 79 per cent nitrogen. At atmospheric pressure nitrogen has no adverse effect on us but when five times as much air as normal enters the body at a depth of 40 metres this means that the blood is absorbing five times as much nitrogen. This increasing concentration of nitrogen with depth in the blood acts as a narcotic, producing the effect known as nitrogen narcosis. Most divers will experience nitrogen narcosis to some degree on the *Rondo*, depending of course on the depth they dive to. For some the narcosis starts at about 25 metres down. For others it can be up to 35 metres. The effect is very subtle and most divers will not be aware that they are suffering. Different people react in different ways to narcosis. For some it is just a feeling of being light-headed; for others it can be frighteningly intense. In extreme cases divers have been known to take their regulators out of their mouths, behave very strangely or indeed lose consciousness. The narcosis is quickly and easily relieved by simply surfacing to the level at which you were affected in the first place, be it 25 or 35 metres. It is as well to remind divers about this because of the depth of the *Rondo*: over the years there have been some very strange goings on at the bows.

Essential Information

Boat launch site: Oban. Gallanach pier. Lochaline pier, Morvern. Tobermory harbour.

Tidal conditions: 0.7 knots maximum. Dive at slack.

Tidal constraints: Tobermory −0500 Dover, +0020 Oban. Salen −0455 Dover, +0025 Oban.

Visibility: 10–15 metres average.

Maximum depth: 52 metres.

Coastguard: Oban (0631) 63720/9.

Police: Tobermory (0688) 2016. Craignure (068 02) 322.

Recompression chambers: Dunstaffanage Marine Laboratory, Oban (0631) 62244. Underwater Training Centre, Fort William (0397) 703786.

Air supplies: Seafare, Portmore Place, Tobermory (0688) 2277. Oban Divers, Laggan, Glenshalloch, Oban (0631) 62755. (Automatic coin-operated.) Lochaline Dive Centre (0967) 421662. (Automatic coin-operated.)

Hydrographic chart: No. 2390, Sound of Mull.

Sea area: Malin.

Position: Lat 56 32 16.5 N Long 05 54 40.0 W.

THE *BREDA*
Ardmucknish Bay,
Oban, West Scotland

The steamship *Breda* is perhaps one of Scotland's most famous and most popular wrecks, a wreck that is visited by most UK divers at some stage of their careers. She sits upright on an even keel in a sheltered bay near Oban, is easily dived and very safe. Couple this with good visibility and a photogenic, structurally intact large wreck and you can see why.

The *Breda* was a steel steamer measuring 402.6 feet in length, with a beam of 58.3 feet and a draught of 34.7 feet. Her gross tonnage was 6,941 and her net tonnage, 4,387. The *Breda* had three deck levels, a cruiser stern and a flat bottom. She was built in 1921 by the New Waterway Shipbuilding Co. at Schiedam, just south of Rotterdam in the Netherlands, for Koninkl Nederl. Stoomb. Maats NV, the Royal Netherlands Steamship Co. She was registered in Amsterdam and the Dutch flag flew from her mast. Her power was generated by four boilers and although these were originally coal-fired she was also fitted for oil fuel and eventually, in 1938, the conversion to oil was made. The boilers fed two double-reduction steam turbines built by Met-Vickers Elec Co. Ltd of Manchester and were geared to a single eight-and-a-half ton manganese bronze propeller which combined to give the *Breda* a service speed of 11.8 knots. Her boilers consumed on average 57 tons of coal or 36 tons of oil in any one 24-hour period. She had a coal capacity in her permanent bunker of 370 tons; her two side bunkers, located dead amidships, gave another 370 tons capacity; and her spare bunker, located near the stern just aft of the mainmast, gave another 190 tons capacity. Her double bottoms were used for storage of oil and had a capacity of 807 tons. From her keel to the top of her foremast she measured 117 feet six inches. She carried a crew of 37 and had accommodation aboard for 16 passengers. She was indeed a mighty vessel.

The *Breda* boasted two large, distinctive goal-post masts, one forward and one aft of the bridge superstructure, and from these at various angles ran off several derricks with block and tackles shackled to them. Dotted around the vessel were ten other squatter, sturdier masts, again with derricks and pulleys designed to load and disgorge cargo from her holds. Two were set side by side at the bow, two in front of the bridge

superstructure, two amidships and the remaining four, fore and aft of the mainmast. In total she had four derricks capable of lifting ten tons, one movable heavy derrick capable of lifting 40 tons, four seven-ton derricks, twelve five-ton derricks and two one-ton derricks. Twenty attendant winches were set around the deck to operate the derrick systems.

The SS *Breda* (courtesy Mr Loet Steeman)

Below decks most of her space was available for storage of cargo. At the bow were two storerooms, one above the other. The remainder of the vessel, with the exception of her engine-rooms, was taken up by her five cavernous holds. Each hold plunged down below decks for three deck levels to the ship's double bottoms. The engine-room was located aft of hold No 3 as was the large single funnel, distinctive because of the two white bands that ran round it, breaking up its otherwise dark appearance. The bridge superstructure was situated between the hold Nos 2 and 3, housing the radio and navigation rooms, officers' accommodation and the passenger accommodation. At either side of the deck-housing here was a covered walkway which ran beneath a glazed observation deck. Aft of the funnel a single lifeboat was suspended in its davit at either side of the hull. Two further lifeboats, making up the full quota of four, were suspended in their davits, one at either side of the single storey deck-house at the stern which housed the accommodation for the crew of 37. On the decking above this structure was the emergency steering position. On the outbreak of World War II a platform was built over this deck-house on which was mounted a heavy stern gun.

For nearly 20 years the *Breda* served her owners well, normally plying

the well-worn route across the stormy waters between Europe and South
America. Her service speed was a steady 11.8 knots and she proved to be
a seaworthy and secure vessel. Like so many trusty merchant vessels, the
dark early days of World War II would see a sudden end to her seagoing
career.

In the early days of World War II the Luftwaffe used their fleets of
distinctive Heinkel 111 bombers to strike at British targets with some
success. Made distinctive by their completely glazed nose cone, they gave
their pilots unrivalled all-round visibility. They were, however, perhaps
the most vulnerable of the Luftwaffe's bombers and during the Battle of
Britain many fell victim to the defensive British fighters, most notably
when they were caught without a fighter screen of Messerschmitt Me109s.
Vulnerable and unable to defend themselves well, they were easy prey for
the fast, manoeuvrable RAF fighters. After the decisive events of the Battle
of Britain their shortcomings were realised. They were rarely used for
daytime attacks and were generally confined to a night-bombing role. By
the end of 1940 only a few daring daylight raids were made against the
British mainland. It was one such daylight raid that would send the *Breda*
to her doom in the depths of Ardmucknish Bay.

On 23 December 1940 a small group of Heinkel 111s took off from
their base at Stavanger in German-occupied Norway just before three

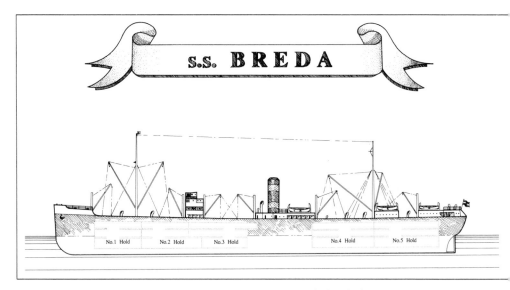

S.S. BREDA

No.1 Hold   No.2 Hold   No.3 Hold   No.4 Hold   No.5 Hold

p.m. Laden with bombs, they struggled into the air and slowly began to climb to the maximum height they could achieve with their deadly cargo, 16,400 feet. Each Heinkel carried four 551-lb bombs nose up in its bomb bay and two larger 1,102-lb bombs on the outside tracks. Twenty minutes later they reached their cruising height of 16,400 feet and set course for Scotland. At their fully laden speed of 193 mph they would take just under three hours to reach their target area, the gathering point for Allied convoys, the Oban Roads on the west coast of Scotland.

When war broke out the *Breda*, although a Dutch cargo vessel, was under the control of the P & O Line. The cruel hand of fate had decreed that she would be in the Oban Roads gathering with many other vessels to be formed up into convoys. The Oban Roads is one of the deepest stretches of sheltered water around Britain's shores and had been chosen as a gathering point for convoys because its great depth made it safe from any enemy attempts to lay mines.

Normally mines were laid with some form of anchorage to the seabed. The British system was that the mines would be pushed off the minelayer on the squat, heavy trolleys used to move the mines around the vessel. The mine was attached to the trolley by a cable cut to the right length for the depth of water the mines were to be laid in. When the mine and its trolley hit the water the trolley sank to the bottom and acted as an anchor mooring the mine in its correct position. The length of cable would be adjusted on the vessel so that the mine, which was positively buoyant, would be suspended at a depth of about 10 metres. This was deep enough so that it would not be wasted by being detonated by a small coastal craft but would catch the bigger vessels with their larger draught. The Oban Roads were so deep that it was impossible to anchor any mines in this fashion.

General arrangement of the SS *Breda*

Opposite: A flight of Heinkel 111's streaked towards the Allied convoy gathering in the Oban Roads (courtesy Imperial War Museum)

The *Breda* had set out for the Oban Roads from London on 12 December on a circuitous route that would eventually take her to Mombassa, Bombay and Karachi. She had reached Oban eight days later on 20 December and took up her position in the Oban Roads. In her five holds she carried a general, mixed cargo: 3,000 tons of cement, 175 tons of tobacco and cigarettes, three Hawker biplanes, 30 De Havilland Moths, spare parts for the aircraft, rubber-soled sandals, military lorry spares, NAAFI crockery, copper ingots, nine dogs and ten horses rumoured to have belonged to the Aga Khan. The merchantmen, *Flynderborg, Dan Y Bryn, Tuva* and the *Lupina*, an Admiralty drifter, were all lying nearby.

Suddenly and without warning at about 5.45 p.m., the seamen on the vessels heard the unfamiliar drone of German aircraft engines as the flight of Heinkel 111s quickly closed in on the ships below. At 193 mph they flashed overhead, swarming over the skies. The ships at anchor below were taken completely by surprise. The speed of the attack had been so fast that no air-raid warning was sounded and the crews of the vessels did not even have time to reach, arm and fire their anti-aircraft guns in defence. The Heinkels had a clear run at the large, stationary merchantmen below them and they were easy targets for the experienced German bomb aimers. Those bombs that missed their target sent great plumes of water rising high into the air to fall back down in a torrent, drenching the ships nearby.

The *Dan Y Bryn* was hit by fragments from a bomb that exploded close to her. The *Tuva* was hit by a bomb in the engine-room and started drifting towards the shore. The *Flynderborg* was hit by a bomb that penetrated in to her bunkers but which mercifully failed to detonate. She was then raked by 7.9 mm machine-gun fire. The Admiralty drifter *Lupina* took a near miss but was damaged so badly that her master was forced to leave her anchorage in a desperate attempt to beach her before she sunk in deep water. At least that way the ship would be saved.

The pilot of one Heinkel picked out the *Breda* as his target and sent his plane streaking towards the huge vessel. A stick of four 551-lb bombs was loosed by the bomb aimer right on target. The German aircrew watched with anticipation as the bombs dropped tail first from the bomb bay before turning to plummet through the air down towards the helpless merchantman. At first it looked as though the attack would result in a direct hit which would cause catastrophic damage and take many lives. Fortune, however, was about to smile on the *Breda* for although the stick of four bombs straddled the vessel, there was no catastrophic direct hit. The bombs exploded in the close vicinity of the ship with such force that the whole vessel shook. The blast fractured internal piping and in the engine-room a cooling water inlet pipe was sheared off. Tons of seawater started to flood into the engine-room and within a few moments the water had killed all steam and the ship's electrics. The *Breda* was dead in the water. Seawater poured with unrelenting fury into the stricken vessel and within minutes the *Breda* was sinking by the stern and developing a list to starboard. As quickly as they had appeared, the Heinkels, having dropped their deadly cargoes, turned and streaked back towards safety in Norway.

Some 15 minutes later, at about six p.m., Captain Johannis Fooy ordered a lifeboat lowered. The *Breda*'s passengers who had all thankfully survived the bombing run were boarded into the lifeboat and ordered to make for the shore. An Admiralty tug came alongside at about 6.15 p.m. and took the *Breda* in tow, heading eastwards towards the shallower water of Ardmucknish Bay. The skipper of the tug realised that the *Breda* was going to sink soon. In a race against time he gambled on running her on to a shallow shelf only six metres deep which extends out to sea from the shore for about 600 metres before dropping off steeply into a depth of 30 metres. If he could beach her both she and her cargo would be saved. If she sunk before he could reach the shelf then the *Breda* and her valuable cargo would be lost and any salvage work made more difficult. It was a desperate race against time.

After towing her for about two hours, at about 8.10 p.m., the tug finally got the *Breda* over the shelf and let go the tow cable. The *Breda*, heavy and low in the water, slowly lost her momentum and came to a shuddering standstill, beaching her bow on the edge of the shelf. The horses were released into the water and allowed to swim ashore. At 8.30 p.m. Captain Fooy and the Chief Mate, the last onboard, abandoned ship. For the time being the immediate danger of losing the ship was over.

With the coming of daylight the next day, Christmas Eve, the Admiralty was able to assess the position. It was felt that the ship was salvageable and some work started immediately. The mighty forces of nature, however, were against the salvagers. Only a fraction of the cargo had been saved when the *Breda*, pounded by the stormy winter seas and pulled by the unseen force of the tide, slid off the shelf into deeper water.

The sinking of the *Breda* would not be the last casualty arising from the daring air-raid. Two or three days after the raid a horse box which had floated free from the *Breda* when she sank had managed to find its way around Kerrera. A Sunderland flying-boat hit it either on take off or landing and sank. It is believed that most of the horses reached the shore safely. The last survivor of the Aga Khan's horses is said to have lived to a ripe old age and died near Oban in 1967.

In 1943 there was some further small-scale salvaging carried out on her by a salvage diver and some copper ingots were recovered. Thereafter she lay in peace, her position marked by her tall goal-post masts which showed at low water. In 1961, at the request of the Northern Lighthouse Board, the Royal Navy swept her with wire to a depth of 28 feet, removing the bridge and funnel and bringing the masts and derricks crashing down on to her submerged decks. Now lost from sight, her memory faded and she was forgotten for the time being.

In 1966 she was 'rediscovered' by sport divers from the Edinburgh branch of the British Sub Aqua Club. Legend has it that the first sport dive on her was made by a solitary diver snorkelling out for nearly a mile from the shore and duckdiving on to her. The secret of her location then became more widely known in diving circles and the wreck started to attract divers in increasing numbers. She was found to be largely intact other than damage caused by small-scale salvaging and the clearance work of 1961.

One of the first salvage divers to start working the wreck was Dave Tye who now runs the popular Oban Divers dive centre at Laggan just outside Oban. Dave Tye had sold up a motorcycle business down in England and moved up to Oban where he started diving for scallops, 'clam diving' as it is known on the west coast. Dave, being a local diver, was asked by the owner of the wreck, Jack O'Neill, to help salvage the eight-and-a-half ton manganese bronze propeller. This was a four-bladed prop, each blade being eight feet high giving a total span of some 16 feet. This sounded relatively straightforward at first but the task was to prove more difficult than envisaged. When he first dived on the wreck Dave found that it was largely intact but nearly 30 years on the bottom had seen the wreck well settled into the soft, silty seabed. When he arrived at the stern he found to his dismay that the prop was completely buried in the seabed.

Initial small-scale excavations soon located the top of one of the blades of the prop three inches under the silt. The bottom of the prop was therefore some 16 feet below the muddy surface. That was a lot of mud

The prop of the *Breda* finally sees the light of day at the South Pier, Oban in 1968. Left to right: Colin Whitton, Dave Tye and Norman O'Neill (courtesy Dave Tye)

to shift as Dave would have to excavate around the prop before it could be blown and lifted to the surface. For a gargantuan task such as this he would need a powerful tool. A home-made airlift was soon constructed to suck away the silt and mud that encased the prop. He also needed manpower to help with the excavation and soon found that there was a never-ending supply of eager amateur divers on hand, all keen to get in on the excitement. Dave would give his customers two free bottles of air, one for helping with the airlift and the other for a free dive on the wreck. The rudimentary airlift was made up of a long tube about six inches in diameter. A compressed air hose served by a compressor on the surface vessel shot compressed air up the tube and this upwards flow of air sucked up silt from the seabed.

Initially the rudimentary airlift was so powerful that on occasions it got sucked into the mud with such force that the divers could not free it. The divers soon found that beneath the mud there was solid clay. The airlift would whistle three feet into the clay and then stick fast. Even attempts to wrench it free by lashing it to the surface vessel, a small fishing boat, and trying to drag it out couldn't pull it clear. The divers were forced to cut the tube where it jutted out from the mud with a hacksaw before they could start reusing it. If a diver got his hand too close to the powerful suction he could find his glove being whipped off his hand to be jettisoned out the top of the airlift.

For six long weeks Dave and his team of volunteer divers dived on the wreck every day. On the surface a long plume of muddy water spewing from the top end of the airlift revealed the success they were having in clearing the prop. Diving conditions were primitive by today's standards. The divers soon stirred up the seabed as they made the airlift ready for use. Even before they started the visibility had been reduced to zero. Once the airlift got going it helped to improve the visibility. Cocooned from the cold in Dunlop dry suits they did not have the luxury of contents gauges to tell them how much air was left in their tanks. Their Snark Mark I tilt valves, through which they breathed, tightened up with about five minutes' air left to go so that they knew it was time to head for the surface.

Slowly the mighty prop of the *Breda* threw off its shroud of silt, revealing itself for the first time in nearly 30 years. After six hard weeks working the airlift the divers had cleared a pit around the prop down to the shaft at the dead centre of the prop. Dave found that, standing on top of the centre of the prop shaft on the tips of his fins, he could just touch the outermost extremity of the blade.

Once the prop was half cleared Dave brought in a 5,000-gallon petrol tank which had started off its life as the back of a railway wagon and which would now act as a giant lifting bag. A hook was welded on to the bottom of the tank. It could then be lowered into the water and flooded so that it would sink down to the bottom beside the prop.

The divers had found that the rudder itself was three inches away from the back of the large nut that held the prop on. They were not able to

The wreck of the SS
Breda

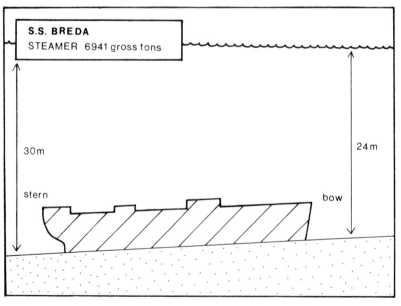

S.S. BREDA
STEAMER 6941 gross tons

30m

stern

24m

bow

get at this nut as it was some considerable distance back under the mud. The plan was to get two of the blades off the prop on one side and two off on the other side by splitting the prop down the middle with explosives. Using air drills the divers shackled the prop to the sunken 5,000-gallon petrol tank. Ten pounds of explosives was placed either side of the centre column of the prop and detonated electrically from the surface vessel. About three-quarters of an hour later, once the mud had started to settle, Dave went down to inspect his handiwork. Through the gloom he found that it had not quite worked out as planned. In fact the prop was intact except for one blade which had been blown completely off!

The divers then made another attempt to cut the shaft by wrapping cortex around it. Again the divers left the water for the safety of the surface vessel and the cortex was blown. Expectantly they kitted up and leapt into the water to find out what had resulted from this attempt. Down on the wreck they again found that things had gone not quite as planned. The explosion had blown the nut off the end of the shaft but the shaft itself remained infuriatingly intact with only a crack in the hub.

Determined to succeed they then took down 26 lb of explosives and packed this into the crack in the hub, at either side and below and above the hub. Sandbags were packed around the explosives to contain the force of the blast instead of much of the power being dissipated outwards. Once satisfied, the divers returned to the surface vessel and, in Dave's words, stood well clear. With the amount of explosives they were using this time they were expecting quite a display. Surely the *Breda* would yield this time.

The explosives were detonated but instead of the expected water spout there was only a muted whoof and a few bubbles floated up to break the surface. The sandbags had done the trick and contained the blast. Dave kitted up once again and went down to find out what had happened. As he went down, the familiar lines of the stern loomed up in front of him in the gloom. Further down and at last he saw what he had been waiting for. The whole prop had come off and was lying at the side of the hole that they had painstakingly excavated. Another of its blades had been blown off it, leaving only two on the prop itself. In all the hub was some three to four feet long and, despite the magnitude of the explosion, Dave was surprised to find that there was still the same gap of two to three inches between the rudder and the hub.

The 5,000-gallon lifting tank was now filled with water and lowered down to the site. Local divers Colin Whitton and Norman O'Neill had gone down with Dave this time and together they shackled the tank to one of the single blades that had been blown off the prop. They filled the tank with compressed air and stood well back. As soon as it became buoyant the tank rushed to the surface, effortlessly lifting the blade with it. The surface vessel then towed the prop to Oban harbour where it was dropped on the bottom at the south pier. The divers then returned to the wreck site to repeat the process with the other single blade and the hub with its two blades still on it.

At Oban harbour the owner of the wreck, Jack O'Neill, had brought in a crane. The prop was shackled up and lifted up on to the pier itself, seeing the light of day for the first time in nearly 30 years. The pieces of the prop were then loaded on to a low-loader and taken to Glasgow for scrapping, realising about £2,500.

Dave Tye also salvaged the valuable degauzing material from the wreck. Degauzing material was made up of about 38 strands of copper wire, each about half an inch in diameter. The material ran around the entire vessel, inside the hull. Its purpose was to demagnetise the ship so that a magnetic mine nearby would not be detonated by the vessel's normal magnetic field. Working in pitch blackness inside the hull, Dave would work by touch alone, feeling his way around the hull until he located the degauzing material. He would then pull it out from the edge of the hull, putting a rope around it and attaching a buoy. In the inky blackness he would then measure out two arm's lengths of the material each way from this buoy and then cut it at either extremity. A buoy would be attached to mark the cut areas and he would then pull each of the 38 copper strands out individually from the cut section, coiling up each strand and putting it into a sack. When he had two or three full sacks they would then be lifted to the surface and towed ashore. Once back at Laggan he would then set fire to the wire to clean off all the insulation and oil from it.

The wreck subsequently passed to new owners who brought in a steam trawler and continued salvaging the valuable parts from the wreck. Soon the condensers and other non-ferrous engine-room fitments had been lifted from the wreck. Further blasting has removed the remaining superstructure, making the lower decks and engine-room more accessible to divers. In 1975 the Royal Navy succeeded without explosives in raising three De Havilland Tiger Moth engines from hold Nos 1 and 2. Since then there has been extensive sport diving on the wreck and many smaller items recovered from the holds. Rubber-soled sandals are always being brought to the surface and many interesting finds have been made in the silty holds. One diver, rummaging about in the bottom of a hold, saw what looked like an old celluloid film sticking out of the hold. He was able to remove it carefully and found that it was a complete archive newsreel with the individual frames easily discernible even after 50 years immersion in the sea. The footage revealed a propaganda-type newsreel of columns of troops with artillery marching through crowded streets.

Today the wreck of the *Breda* lies in the sheltered waters of Ardmucknish Bay in position Lat 56 28 33.0 N and Long 05 25 00.0 W. Once the furious winter seas had driven and sucked the *Breda* off the six-metre-deep shelf, she slid backwards on an even keel down into deeper water. She came to rest on a gentle slope with her stern in 30 metres of water and her bow in 24 metres.

The *Breda* is best dived from RIBs and it is usually and conveniently marked with three buoys, one at the stern, one amidships and one at the bow, enabling you to choose on which section of the wreck you wish to dive. These buoys are sturdy and well secured to the wreck and it is quite safe to tie your boat on to them whilst your divers are down. Her bows, in the shallower water, point towards the shores of Ardmucknish almost a mile away. There are a number of launch sites for your RIB. Launching is possible at Dunstaffanage, or Ledaig in Ardmucknish Bay. If you are staying at Oban Divers dive centre at Laggan, Glenshalloch just south of Oban, you can launch at the slip at Gallanach pier about two miles south of Oban on the unclassified coast road. Divers are welcomed and encouraged here and it is a RIB trip of about 25 minutes up the coast to the site.

Visibility down on the wreck is quite variable as the Bay is very silty and bad weather can stir the bottom up considerably. Average visibility is around 8 to 10 metres and a good day will see 15 metres visibility.

The *Breda* sits on an even keel on a soft, silty seabed. When Dave Tye of Oban Divers was salvaging her prop in 1968 he found that the *Breda* was settled into the seabed to such an extent that the topmost blade of the prop was about three inches beneath the seabed. Twenty-five years later the *Breda* is even further settled into the silt with a drop of only about eight metres from her main deck to the seabed.

The *Breda* was built with one purpose in mind: carrying cargo, and was designed to maximise the load she could carry. As a result, other than her engine-rooms and a few storerooms, her below decks space was completely given over to accommodate her five large holds. Her crew were housed in the stern superstructure and her captain, officers and passengers in the midships superstructure which held the bridge. Dotted around the main deck were other smaller superstructures each given over for a specific purpose. At either side of the hull in between hold Nos 4 and 5 were two small deck-houses dotted with portholes. The starboard side deck-house held the galley and the port-side, WCs. The cooks and engineers were housed separately in two further deck-houses, one either side of the main deck just forward of hold No 4. The clearance work in 1961 resulted in the removal of her two distinctive goal-post masts and her midships superstructure was almost completely blasted off, removing the bridge. The remnants of this superstructure now are a tangled mass rising at most about one level above the main deck. The other small superstructures were left untouched but the long immersion in the sea has caused them to deteriorate severely. The roofs and walls have almost completely rotted away, leaving only a framework of ribs through which divers can swim. The stern superstructure is the only structure which rises up two levels above the main deck. All over the deck lie the massive tubular steel derricks and ventilator funnels which were brought crashing down on to the deck by the clearance works.

At the very bow a large section of the hull has been cut away almost to the seabed and removed. This section held the raised fo'c'sle storerooms superstructure and, below decks, more storerooms. As you move aft, however, the vessel soon takes on a recognisable ship shape, her graceful lines disappearing into the distance. At either side of the hull a raised bulwark rail, some three feet high and punctuated by drainage gaps, defines the width of her deck and runs the whole length of the ship. Her wooden deck planking has, at this foremost section, rotted away to reveal the structural cross-members. A large derrick with its smaller jib still attached has been brought crashing down on to the deck and now points fore and aft, jutting out over the void between the sheared deck and the remnants of the bow far below. Moving aft, hold No 1 appears, deeply filled with silt. Between it and hold No 2 the jagged remains of the foremost goal-post masts can be made out.

Hold No 2 is again well filled with silt but against the aftmost bulkhead, boots, sandals and tyres can be found. On the main deck to the starboard side lie the rotted and collapsed remains of a truck, instantly recognisable by its four large, rugged tyres. The framework of its drive system and axles can still be made out. Aft of this hold the devastated remains of the superstructure which formerly held the bridge can be found. This superstructure originally rose up some four levels above the main deck but the blasting and clearance works have left only parts of the lower deck intact. The forward bulkhead is still recognisable with its row of portholes. Behind this, however, the innards of this deck-house are now a confused jumble of jagged and twisted plates of steel.

Behind the confusion of this devastated superstructure the 58-feet wide expanse of the main deck reforms. At either side are small hatches allowing access below decks, the starboard hatch having a fallen derrick lying over it. The lip of the hatch is buckled from the impact as the derrick crashed down during the 1961 clearance operations. Further aft and hold No 3 appears, situated between the bridge and the smaller midships superstructure which was formerly dominated by the funnel. This hold held her cargo of aircraft which has now been removed. Several spare engines are still in this hold and there have been attempts recently to salvage them. A large, fallen tubular steel derrick straddles this hold, running from the back of the bridge right back to this midships superstructure.

This second piece of superstructure is more intact than the bridge area and is easily recognisable for what it was. It rises up one deck level only and originally housed the bunkers in the centre and, at either side, the cooks' and engineers' deck-houses. A covered walkway ran down the side of these deck-houses and this has now rotted away, leaving only the structural struts that gave it strength. The engine-room, turbines and boiler-rooms were located immediately below decks in this area. In the centre of this superstructure there is a cavernous round hole which marks the spot where the distinctive banded funnel once stood. It has long since rotted away and collapsed. Two wooden lifeboats originally swung in davits above this superstructure at either side of the hull but they are long since gone.

Aft of this superstructure the cavernous void of hold No 4 appears. Like the others this is well filled with silt but the topmost part of its cargo of brooms and cigarette tins can still be made out. At the forward end of the hold a ladder rises out of the silt, spanning the gap between the silt and the underside of the main deck. Steel rungs are welded on to the rim of the hold above it, allowing the crew access into the hold. The starboard derrick which stood just behind the bulkhead of the superstructure has been brought crashing down by the clearance works and now lies across the open hold. The port side derrick has also been brought down but it fell over the side of the vessel. It now stands upright on the seabed below, resting against the hull and projecting up above the bulwark rail.

Between hold Nos 4 and 5 are the two smaller deck-houses which housed the galley and the WCs. The roof of the WCs has gone and the walls of the starboard side galley have rotted away completely, leaving a latticework of struts through which it is possible to swim easily.

Hold No 5, the last hold, now appears. Although half filled with silt there is still a considerable drop from the main deck down into it. The bottom of the hold is strewn with spare Army lorry parts, such as the coils of shock absorbers, bottles and solidified bags of cement. The forward bulkhead of this hold is a complete wall of solidified bags of cement, all still neatly stacked in place. On the port side of this hold a large tubular steel derrick and its attached smaller jib have been brought down. The derrick rests jutting out over the side of the hull and runs fore and aft. The jib lies on the deck beside it. The *Breda* had a number of large steel ventilator funnels that rose up from the cargo spaces below, through the main deck. One of these has broken in two, the top part now having fallen on to the deck here.

Aft of hold No 5 the stern superstructure rises up from the deck, its forward bulkhead lined with a row of portholes and doors. The wooden deck planking of the roof of this deck-house is still in place. At either side of the central deck-house itself were two smaller deck-houses, again with their outmost bulkheads flush with the bulwark rail and dotted with a row of portholes. The port side deck-house held the WCs and the starboard side, washrooms. These deck-houses were effectively connected to the central deck-house by a covered walkway from which doorways opened into the deck-houses on either side. Two wooden lifeboats originally swung in their davits here but the lifeboats are long gone as are the roofs of these deck-houses, making them safe and easy for divers to enter.

At the very stern of the *Breda*, flush with the curved stern itself, sits the superstructure that housed the steering. On the port side two portholes and a doorway allow an insight into this deck-house. In the stern photograph of the vessel a circular winch, used for weighing mooring ropes, can be seen mounted on a column beside two hawses. This winch has now fallen from its mount and sits on the small section of deck aft of the WCs. In this same photograph this deck-house can be seen to rise up to only one level above the main deck. Divers diving this wreck today will notice that this stern deck-house is in fact the only piece of superstructure left on the wreck which rises up to two deck levels. This is a pre-war photograph of the *Breda*, for at the beginning of World War II a gun platform was constructed above the one-level deck-house. The sides of this deck-house have now rotted away, allowing easy entry for divers. In the centre a large circular column runs from the roof down into the deck below, possibly part of a wracking sytem for the gun. The gun itself was removed some time ago, it is thought, by Royal Navy divers.

The *Breda* is a classic wreck dive. Her very size is dominating and takes some time to appreciate. She is an exciting but safe wreck dive. Her holds and superstructure are open and accessible but, above all, safe. There is no appreciable current to worry about. Her relatively shallow depth means that a diver's bottom time is not too limited and a considerable time can be spent down on her, taking in her fine lines and dimensions. Although she has necessarily suffered as a result of the clearance operations on her and her long immersion in the sea, she is still a scenic dive, well populated by schools of fish. For these reasons she is a very popular first wreck dive for many divers. Novice divers can drift along her walkways, peering in through portholes, or drop down into her cavernous holds to rummage amongst the silt and debris. The wreck of the *Breda* graces most UK divers' logbooks at some stage of their diving careers. She is without doubt one of Scotland's greatest wrecks.

Essential Information

Boat launch site: Oban, Gallanach pier. Dunstaffanage or Ledaig.
Tidal conditions: 0–0.2 knots.
Visibility: 5–15 metres.
Maximum depth: Deck 15 metres. Holds 20 metres. Seabed, bow 24 metres, stern 30 metres.
Coastguard: Oban (0631) 63720/9.
Police: Oban (0631) 62213.
Air supplies: Oban Divers, Laggan, Glenshalloch, Oban (0631) 62755.
Recompression chamber: Dunstaffanage Marine Laboratory, Oban (0631) 62244.
Sea area: Malin.
Hydrographic chart: No 2378 Loch Linnhe.
Position: Lat 56 28 33.0 N, Long 05 25 00.0 W.

HMS *PORT NAPIER*
Loch Alsh, West Scotland

The wreck of HMS *Port Napier* lies in about 20 metres of water in Loch Alsh, the narrow stretch of sea that separates the Isle of Skye from the mainland of north-west Scotland. She is one of Scotland's best loved and most visited wrecks, known to most British divers. Practically every day, one or more dive boats will make the short ten-minute trip out from Kyle of Lochalsh on the mainland to her final resting place. Countless divers are drawn to her year after year. She is a fascinating wreck and holds something of interest for every grade of diver from novice to advanced.

A variety of factors combine to elevate the wreck of HMS *Port Napier* to the status of one of Scotland's greatest wrecks. The dramatic tale of how she met her end captures the imagination of those who hear it. The wreck is easily accessible, just a short boat trip from both the mainland and Skye itself. She is remarkably well preserved considering the manner in which she met her doom and her long immersion in the sea. Her upmost port side breaks through the surface of the water at low tide and her hull plating here has been removed. Many of her inner spaces are now open to daylight above, allowing a means of escape if a diver runs into trouble and has to ascend. She is therefore an ideal first wreck dive for the novice diver who can feel and experience the sensations of wreck diving in relative safety. Snorkellers, too, are able to drift round the wreck, getting a good feel for its size and layout, perhaps watching their fellow divers exploring the deeper areas below them. The more experienced diver will find the deeper areas of HMS *Port Napier* challenging and will be able to penetrate and explore the innards of this mighty vessel.

The wreck of HMS *Port Napier* lies well out of the main tidal stream in the loch and there are consequently no dangerous currents to tug divers away from the wreck, separating them from their surface boat cover. This area boasts relatively good average visibility and the wreck itself is abundantly covered with sponges, hydroids and anemones. Like any wreck, it has become an artificial reef, attracting colonies of fish which can find food and, in turn, hide from predators in its intricate nooks and crannies. HMS *Port Napier* is indeed the perfect wreck and over the years has been many a diver's first experience of wreck diving.

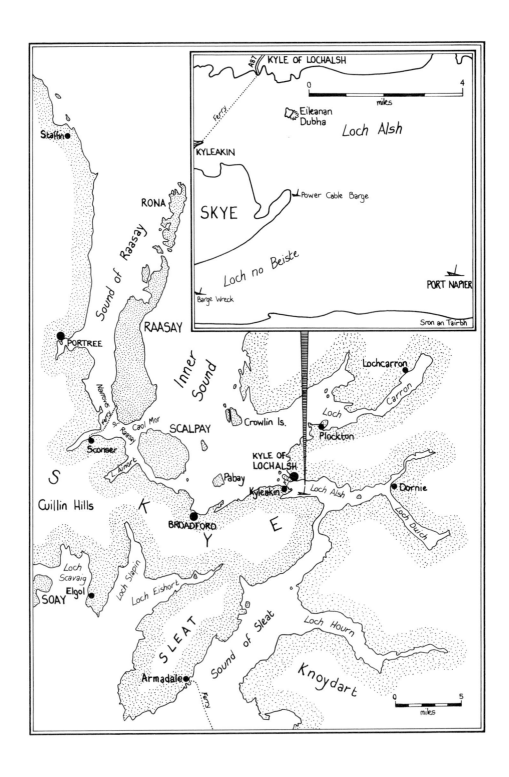

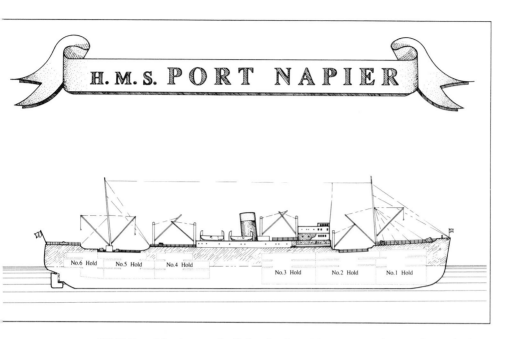

HMS *Port Napier* was built by the Port Line in 1940 during the early days
of World War II but she was requisitioned and taken over by the Ministry
of War Transport, in June 1940 whilst she was still under construction
for conversion to a minelayer. The Port Line grew from humble beginnings
before World War I into a major shipping line between the wars but
ultimately was devastated by heavy shipping losses in World War II.

Initially the fledgling Port Line entered into several successful joint
ventures with other shipping lines and rapidly expanded in size. At the
end of World War I the Canadian Government formed a company,
Canadian Merchant Marine Ltd, to trade between the eastern seaboard
of Canada and Australasia. The venture unfortunately proved to be a
commercial disaster and the service failed and was discontinued. The Port
Line filled the void by entering into a joint venture with the New Zealand
Shipping Co. Ltd and the Ellerman and Bucknall Steamship Co. Ltd, each
owning equal shares. The partnership started up the Montreal, Australia
and New Zealand Line to replace the failed Canadian Merchant Marine
service. The many and varied talents of the three different shipping lines
fused well and made the venture a commercial success. The Port Line
built three vessels specifically for this service, the *Port Halifax, Port Saint
John* and *Port Montreal*. In 1939 they added the *Port Quebec* to their
fleet, this being the first time that the Port Line had used Canadian names
for their ships.

By the outbreak of World War II the Port Line had expanded to a
total of 14 steamers and 14 motorships, all constructed to the highest
specifications and boasting above-average speeds, essential in wartime. A

great number of these vessels were taken over by the Admiralty for war service but despite their great speed, many of the Port Line's fleet were lost through enemy action. The first casualty was the *Port Denison* which was bombed and sunk off the Aberdeenshire coast of Scotland in September 1940. On 11 October 1940 the *Port Gisborne* was sunk by U-boat torpedoes in the Atlantic. The next to fall was the *Port Brisbane* which was sunk on 21 November 1940 by the enemy surface raider *Pinguin* in the South Indian Ocean. On 24 November 1940 the motorship *Port Hobart* was sunk by the colossal firepower of the big guns of the German pocket battleship *Admiral Scheer* off Bermuda. In rapid succession other losses followed. On 27 November 1940 HMS *Port Napier* herself was lost and then, only a few days later, on 30 November 1940 the *Port Wellington* was sunk in the South Indian Ocean by the *Pinguin*, which had sunk the *Port Brisbane* just nine days earlier. In two short months the Port Line had lost six fine vessels, taking many brave seamen to their graves.

In 1941 the rate of attrition slowed down and only two vessels were lost. On 3 March the *Port Townsville* was bombed and sunk in the Bristol Channel. On 28 April the *Port Hardy* was torpedoed and lost whilst on an Atlantic convoy. During 1942 three Port Line vessels were lost. On 10 June the *Port Montreal* was torpedoed in the Caribbean and six days later, on 16 June, the *Port Nicholson* was sunk in an Atlantic convoy. The *Port Hunter* was torpedoed off the coast of Sierra Leone on 11 July. The last Port Line losses came during 1943. On 17 March in the North Atlantic the *Port Auckland* fell prey to a prowling U-boat which successfully attacked and torpedoed her. On 30 April the *Port Victor* also fell victim to U-boat attack in the same area.

HMS *Port Napier* was a substantial vessel with a gross weight of 9,600 tons. She measured 498 feet and three inches in length with a beam of 68 feet and a depth to the upper or main deck of 41 feet and six inches. Her original peacetime design was modified fairly extensively to meet the Admiralty's requirements for her use as a minelayer. The area where her holds were was completely decked over, the only exception being a loading hatch near the stern for her deadly cargo of 550 mines. She was fitted out with an array of defensive firepower although it was hoped that this would not be needed as she was intended to operate under the cover of the main fleets. Two four-inch guns were mounted singly, side by side on her bow. Four 20 mm anti-aircraft guns were mounted amidships and in addition she was fitted with two single two-pounder anti-aircraft guns and two five-inch anti-aircraft guns. Four minelaying doors were cut into her curved stern and narrow-gauge railways were laid in corridors linking these doors with her holds where her cargo of mines would be stored. The heavy mines were set on trolleys which could be moved around the vessel on these rails.

Nearly every vessel that can float can be adapted to lay mines and because of this the Admiralty held off constructing purpose-built naval minelayers in peacetime. The Admiralty recognised that for laying mines in enemy waters, speed was vital and this consideration was given greater importance than the number of mines that could be carried. For laying mines in areas outwith enemy control the exact opposite was true: it was the payload that could be carried and deployed that was important. When war broke out the Admiralty immediately put in hand the construction of new fast cruiser minelayers and destroyers designed to lay mines in enemy territory. In addition many merchant vessels such as the *Port Napier* were requisitioned for conversion for a minelaying role in safer waters. (The RAF had minelaying aircraft which were used for minelaying deep in enemy waters. Of the 300,000 mines laid by British forces during the war, about 20 per cent were laid from the air, in areas inaccessible for surface vessels.)

The newly converted HMS *Port Napier* was one of many mercantile vessels with a large radius of action and capable of carrying large quantities of mines. These vessels were used to lay mine barrages in areas which were relatively safe from the threat of enemy action. HMS *Port Napier* formed part of the 1st Minelaying squadron that operated from 1940 to 1943 based in port 'ZA' (Scotland). The 1st Minelaying squadron was detailed to mine the western approaches to the British Isles and consisted of the auxiliary minelayers *Agamemnon*, *Menetheus*, *Port Quebec* and *Southern Prince* supplemented at times by one or more of the naval cruiser minelayers. HMS *Port Napier*, however, was not destined to survive for long in the war. Her career up to her sinking would be so short that she was not even recorded in the Register of Ships at Lloyds.

On the night of 27 November 1940 HMS *Port Napier* was berthed alongside the pier at Kyle of Lochalsh, a deep mooring which could easily accommodate a vessel of her size. Because of its good docks and its railhead, Kyle of Lochalsh had quickly become a significant naval base. Ratings had been hard at work unloading the 550 mines destined for HMS *Port Napier* which had arrived by rail. For days her crew had, in turn, laboured hard, carefully loading the dangerous cargo of mines down through the small loading hatch in the deck near the stern. From there the crew ran the mines along narrow-gauge rails inside the vessel before stationing them in the six cavernous decked-over holds. Their task was now nearly complete: her full complement of mines was onboard as were 6,000 rounds of ammunition for her guns.

The loading operation had gone smoothly until suddenly someone spotted that a fire had broken out aboard her. At first frantic attempts were made to extinguish the flames, but without success. Despite the efforts of the firefighters the flames spread remorselessly and it soon became apparent to those aboard that the fire could not be controlled. A red glow grew in intensity, lighting up the darkness of the night sky. The intensity of the fire grew and grew as did the realisation that if the fires reached her cargo there would be a cataclysmic explosion that would level Kyle.

As a result of the growing danger to the town the priority now became to get the burning vessel as far away as possible. The fire could not be extinguished and would now be allowed to run its full course. Only time would tell what the outcome would be. Many of the residents of Kyle noticed the fire and general commotion down at the pier and congregated at the dock, curious to see what was going on. As they pressed forward to watch the fire they had to be held back by police. To protect the inhabitants and buildings of the town frantic arrangements were made for Kyle to be evacuated. HMS *Port Napier* was cast loose from her moorings and taken in tow away from the town initially, of necessity, in the direction of the small village of Kyleakin on the other side of Loch Alsh on Skye. Hurried plans were made for the inhabitants of Portree, Skye's main town, 30 miles to the north, to take in the evacuees from Kyleakin, although the evacuation was never put into effect. Whilst under tow the fires continued to intensify and eventually in Loch no Beiste, a small bay about a mile east of Kyleakin and well away from habitation, the burning vessel was let loose and cast adrift.

Shortly afterwards there was a loud explosion which resonated around the nearby hills of Skye and a flash that lit up the night sky momentarily. Part of the central superstructure was blown off the vessel several hundred feet into the air and all the way to the shores of Skye about a quarter of a mile away. The superstructure landed on the beach, complete with one gun mounting and a bath. Some of the fragments even ended up halfway up the hill beyond where they still sit among the trees.

Surprisingly, despite the magnitude of the explosion that blew part of the superstructure off her, none of the mines were detonated although her midships was mangled by the explosion. The *Port Napier* rapidly flooded with water and keeled over to her starboard side. She then slipped beneath the waves and came to rest on her starboard side in about 20 metres of water with her entire cargo of newly loaded mines. Her beam was 68 feet which meant that her port side showed above the water at most states of the tide. That night, because of some German bombing over Ayrshire some 200 miles to the south, a strict security blackout was imposed to keep the loss secret. As a result, nothing appeared in any local or national newspapers. As with many other sea losses in both world wars rumours of sabotage were rife. The security blackout probably fuelled these rumours. In the absence of any official explanation people speculated wildly about what had happened and these rumours became more and more exaggerated as they passed around.

HMS *Port Napier* and her dangerous cargo lay in her watery grave for the remainder of the war. Eventually, in 1950 the Royal Navy decided to remove the mines to make the wreck safe. After studying the way she was lying they decided upon a salvage strategy that would unintentionally elevate HMS *Port Napier* to the status of one of Scotland's greatest wrecks. In 1955/6 a Royal Navy salvage team from HMS *Barglow* removed the entire upmost port side plating of her hull, exposing the inner ribs, bulkheads and double bottoms. By doing this they were able to have RN clearance divers rig up a lift system and lift the mines vertically up to the surface between each of the decks. Five hundred and twenty-six mines were removed and 16 had to be detonated *in situ* for safety reasons. Four thousand rounds of ammunition were also recovered. The Admiralty were never sure of the exact number of mines originally on her and have never been convinced that they were able to remove all of them and so they have steadfastly refused to sell the wreck ever since. The propellers have at some stage been removed by unauthorised salvors and applications have been made within the last few years to remove the prop shafts, wire cable and other deck fittings.

Today the wreck of HMS *Port Napier* lies at Latitude 57 15 58.0 N and Longitude 005 41 11.0 W about 330 yards from the shores of Skye. At 498 feet in length she is a big vessel, requiring several dives to fully grasp her layout. Her uppermost port side shows above the waterline at most states of the tide, except high water. With her upper port side hull plating removed it is easy for snorkellers to swim around her decks and explore her innards. For novice divers she is a very safe and yet scenic dive, her first five metres covered with kelp forests that sway slightly in the gentle current. Experienced divers can penetrate the hull in many places, following the rails through the hull, to the four minelaying doors at the stern cut just above the waterline and from where the mine trolleys were pushed out and the mines deployed.

The wreck is easily accessed from either Kyle of Lochalsh itself on the mainland or alternatively, if you are spending time on Skye, from the small ferry port of Kyleakin on the island just a short hop across Loch Alsh. At Kyle divers should use the old ferry slip to launch and retrieve dive boats. This is the small slip running along the curve of the harbour just beneath the main public carpark and immediately to the south of the main ramp where the regular ferry to Skye loads and discharges its vehicular and foot passengers. In no circumstances should the main ramp be used as the commercial ferry comes in quickly and very frequently and divers should avoid hindering its passage. It pays dividends to check the state of the tide here before diving as at low water the water level drops well beneath the end of the slip, making it difficult to launch and nearly impossible to retrieve dive boats. Most divers use the Kyle slip and it is common to find groups of divers from all over the UK kitting up here and getting ready for the trip out to the wreck. It can be a quite sociable place to be with many a diver recounting having seen the 'missing mines'!

Once the divers are ready and loaded into the dive boat it is a short, scenic dash across Loch Alsh towards the rugged hills of Skye. Watch your echo-sounder as you pass over the centre of the sea loch: it gets really deep in the middle. Here in the centre of the tidal race, the current can be fierce. As you cross, however, and get nearer to Skye the current

The wreck of HM
Port Napier

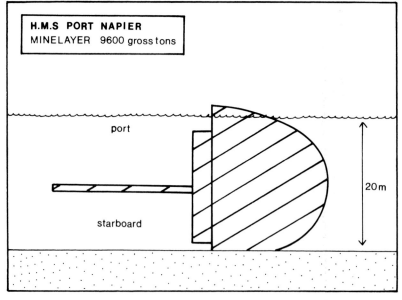

H.M.S PORT NAPIER
MINELAYER   9600 gross tons

port

starboard

20 m

dies off almost completely so that by the time you are in the vicinity of the wreck there will be a maximum current of 0.2 knots. The wreck is easily located at low tide as it stands well clear of the water and provides a good mooring point for the dive boat's painter. On the shore 300 metres away a complete section of deck-housing blown there in the original explosion in 1940 can be made out. For some years now there has been a small buoy attached to the wreck's foremast and this marks her position at high water when she can be completely submerged.

The bow of HMS *Port Napier* lies in about 18 metres of water and her stern in slightly deeper water at 21 metres. She lies on her starboard side on a silty seabed and retains her ship shape completely. Her bow and stern are largely intact but her midships is a bit jumbled although not so as to be unrecognisable. All around her on the seabed are profusions of scallop shells, spars, pieces of plating and general debris from the ship. The seabed is littered with cables, metal chests, pieces of deck gear and, of late, a collection of assorted shoes and boots, presumably as a result of someone breaking open the shoe locker. Some of the shoes even have the wooden insert used to help them keep their shape when being stored still in place. Long shards of kelp adorn most of the structure down to about five metres depth and partially hide the port-side bow gun, making it sometimes difficult to locate. Beneath the line of kelp the wreck is covered with anemones, the soft coral known as dead men's fingers and feather duster worms. Like most wrecks, HMS *Port Napier* has become an artificial reef, home to a wide variety of sealife. As you drift through the wreck you will occasionally bump into a large, solitary cod eyeing you warily. Schools of saithe will flash past you and if you are lucky a seal or two may come in close for a look at the unusually cumbersome and noisy visitor to its underwater world.

Visibility will be about ten metres or more on average, depending on the time of year and the prevailing weather conditions. The visibility never seems to close down completely on this wreck no matter how bad the conditions are.

Most dives on HMS *Port Napier* start by mooring to the buoy attached to the foremast. The mooring rope for the buoy makes a convenient guide to follow down until you reach the foremast at about eight metres down. The mast has a rich, rough covering of marine growth over it and swathes of kelp and cross rigging hang down from it. The foremast runs off horizontally towards the wreck itself, only barely discernible at this distance as a dark mass in the distance. Finning along the mast towards the wreck, you arrive at the forward superstructure. At the back of this are three doorways set one above the other leading into the superstructure. The topmost doorway was obviously the switch room as the walls are still covered with junctions and wiring. The rooms are heavily filled with silt and too tight for a diver to enter.

Moving forward from this section of superstructure, the wooden deck planking is still visible. Not far ahead stand the two four-inch guns.

Originally mounted side by side, they now lie one above the other and are still in good condition, their barrels still pointing defiantly out over the bow. The shallowest port-side gun is in about five metres of water and is covered in kelp. The deeper gun is in about 12 metres and is free of kelp. It is in pristine condition and makes an excellent photographic subject. Just forward of the two guns are the electric windlasses for weighing the forward anchors. Anchor chains run out along the deck before disappearing through the anchor hawsepipes. The starboard anchor chain is run out, dropping through its hawsepipe to the seabed below. Further forward and the tip of the bow is reached with its railing still in place. Here on the seabed the soft silty bottom is littered with sea shells and clams and it is quite spectacular to fin under the bow itself and, standing on the seabed, look up to the silhouette of the bow towering above you. Her original design provided for two cargo holds forward of the bridge superstructure. When she was converted by the Admiralty during construction for minelaying these were sealed over with decking and the two four-inch guns are situated on top of what would have been No 2 hold. Of the six holds originally planned, hold Nos 1 to 5 were designed to take insulated frozen cargo. Hold No 6 at the very stern was designated for general cargo. All the holds were divided into three sections, one above the other. The main hold was at the bottom with the lower and upper 'tweens above.

Moving from the bow towards the stern along the seabed you will pass beneath the starboard four-inch gun near where the sweep of the hull from the bow meets the seabed. Here a few portholes are visible, the brass fitments themselves sadly gone. Moving further aft you will pass under the foremast and superstructure where your dive started. Here the seabed is a jumbled mass of plates and spars. There is a large gap where there is only flat decking, covering what was originally hold No 3, before the midships superstructure and mainmast are reached. The superstructure here runs all the way down to the seabed and where it meets the seabed there is a jagged opening easily large enough to allow a diver to enter. If you have a torch then it is possible to go inside the superstructure here and fin the ten metres or so along a companionway to emerge aft of this piece of superstructure. The funnel has rotted and fallen from its mountings to the seabed below.

Behind this superstructure there are several openings by which you can get in to the minelaying corridors. These corridors run for some considerable distance inside the wreck and still have the narrow-gauge railway tracks running along them. On these tracks the trolleys, used to carry the mines, could move from the holds to the minelaying doors at the stern of the vessel. From here they were pushed out lock, stock and barrel when being deployed. These trolleys had two functions. Whilst inside the vessel they were solely for transportation of the mines. To deploy the mine the trolley and its integral mine were pushed out of one of the four minelaying doors. The mine was attached by a cable to the trolley and once deployed the trolley sank and acted as an anchor for the mine. Scattered around on the seabed are a few of the trolleys still with lengths of cable coiled on them.

Further astern and the decked-over hold Nos 5 and 6 are visible. At the vessel's rounded stern are the four clearly visible minelaying doors. This is the exit point for more experienced divers who have swum along the rail corridors inside the vessel and also the starting point for other divers to fin forward inside.

Because it is relatively shallow, divers can now ascend and spend some time exploring the shallower regions of the wreck and effectively use this as a safety decompression period before returning to the dive boat for the short trip back to the slip at Kyle.

The wreck is so large that it will still hold enough of interest for a second dive. You can return to spend some time exploring a particular area that caught your interest on the first dive. Alternatively there are a few smaller wrecks of interest not far away which are great for second dives. In 12 metres of water off a rocky spur that is the westmost edge of Loch no Beiste lies the wreck of a 90-foot barge. It lies about 15 metres out to the south-east of the rocky shore between the point itself and the yellow power cable marker on the rocks. It is easily picked up on an echo-sounder and can be just as easily located if you don't have a sounder, by mooring against the rocks and finning straight out close to the point for about 15 metres south-eastwards until you come upon the wreck rising up from the seabed for about five metres. On the way there you will pass over a seabed that is littered with all sorts of old bottles deposited here over a number of years in much the same fashion as the Bottle Dive in Gutter Sound at Scapa Flow. Presumably this was an old anchorage and these were tossed over the side from vessels moored here in the past.

The barge is obviously quite old and was rediscovered in the early 1980s when a remotely operated vehicle (ROV) was being used to check a sub-sea power cable, the yellow marker for which can be seen on the nearby rocks. It had become clear that there was an underwater obstruction hindering the cable and the ROV was sent down to see what it was. It was then discovered that the cable had been laid over a wreck and it was subsequently repositioned.

The barge sits upright on an even keel. There are deck hatches at the stern and bow although only the one at the stern is open, allowing access into the tight accommodation area. The remainder of the vessel is made up of open, empty cargo space. The covers for this long rectangular area have long gone, leaving the structural support beams crossing it at regular intervals. The cargo space now has a deep layer of silt which is easily disturbed, billowing up in clouds to close down the visibility quickly. This area is, however, usually well populated by small scallops called Queenies which, when disturbed, kick up in numbers and jerk away like false teeth. The innards of the wreck are soon explored and then it is possible to circumnavigate the hull on the seabed. The gap between the hull and the seabed is always packed full of crabs, lobsters and the occasional conger eel. The seabed round about is littered with debris from the wreck and broken and intact old bottles.

In the middle of Loch no Beiste itself lies another wreck of a barge. She too sits on an even keel but is in deeper water of 22 metres. She is of a similar length as the power cable barge, about 80 feet. It is possible to drop down through the deck hatch at the stern and get into the small accommodation area which, again, is a tight fit. Some crockery and an old kettle have been recovered from here. The two forward holds are open and have coal in them. Once again there is a cave-like gap round the hull where it meets the seabed which is home to a wide variety of life and a few conger eels.

Essential Information
Boat launch site: Old ferry slipway, Kyle of Lochalsh or Kyleakin.
Tidal conditions: 0.2 knots maximum.
Visibility: 10–15 metres average.
Maximum depth: 21 metres.
Coastguard: Oban (0631) 63720/9.
Police: Kyle of Lochalsh (0599) 4222.
Recompression chambers: Underwater Training Centre, Fort William (0397) 703786.
Air supplies: Portree Diving Services (0478) 2274. Skye Diving Centre, Harlosh (047) 022 366.
Hydrographic chart: No 2540, Loch Alsh and approaches.
Sea area: Minches.
Position: Lat 57 15 58.0 N, Long 05 41 11.0 W.

THE *WALLACHIA*
Firth of Clyde

The *Wallachia* ranks alongside the mighty *Akka* as one of the most important of the innumerable shipwrecks in the Firth of Clyde. At 259 feet long she can easily be explored in one dive and her fine lines, so distinctive of 19th-century steamships, appreciated. She is a relic from a bygone age, a tantalising glimpse of the majestic days of steam.

When she sank in 1895 the cold, dark waters of the Firth of Clyde closed over her, hiding her final resting place. Soon she had been forgotten about, just one more wrecking to add to the long list of vessels that had come to grief in the Clyde. For nearly 100 years she has lain unsalvaged in the dark, murky depths of the Firth of Clyde. She still carries a treasure trove of artefacts in her six cargo holds, a time capsule that spans the centuries.

At the time of her doom in 1895, she carried a mixed cargo of stannous chloride in two-gallon jars, bottled beer, and general goods bound for the West Indies. Each of the two-gallon stannous chloride jars still bears the inscription on its lid of its maker, 'Richard Smith, Acid Maker, Glasgow', a company still in business today. One of her holds, some 20 feet deep, is filled to just a few feet from its top with hundreds of distinctive dark green/brown beer bottles. When you drop into the beer bottle hold all you see is the top of the pile. Scores of beer bottles, most still with their corks in, stick out from the silt that has settled thickly over the hold and its contents. Many of the beer bottles have been recovered from the wreck, their contents undisturbed . . . but not drinkable. The bottles come in at least four sizes: larger pale ale bottles about a foot high and distinctive smaller bottles for stout. They would have been a welcome taste of home for those early pioneering expatriates working in the tropical climate of the West Indies. Soon after being lifted to the surface the change in pressure results in a stream of bubbles forcing their way up the side of the cork. Like a muted champagne bottle, eventually the cork will be forced out. Many of the corks bear the words 'McEwans Edinburgh' along their sides and look as fresh as the day they were put in. The beer, although not drinkable, still smells distinctly alcoholic even after 100 years at the bottom of the Firth of Clyde. By keeping the bottle cool and

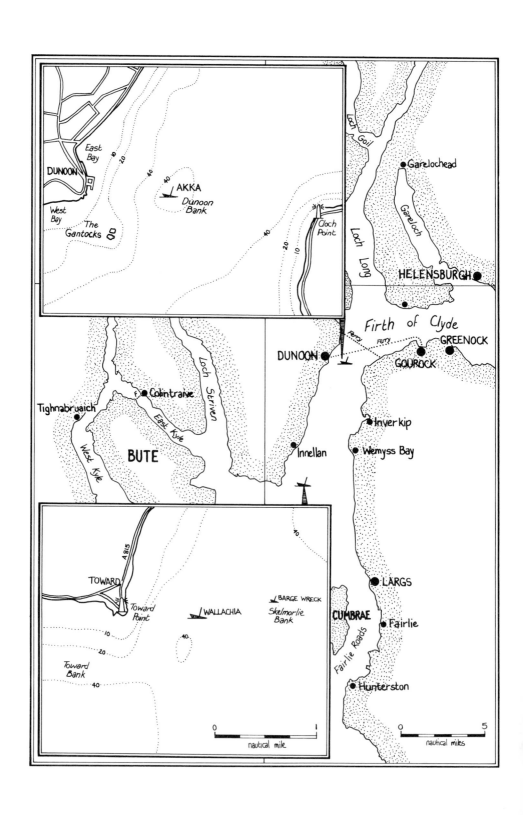

immersed in water it is possible to keep it corked and preserve the contents for posterity.

The *Wallachia* was built by Oswald Mordaunt & Sons in Southampton and launched in March 1883. She was 259.2 feet long with a beam of 36.1 feet and a draught of 18 feet. An iron, single-screw steamship, her gross weight was 1,724 tons, net 1,077 tons and she was registered at Lloyds, No 87830. Her first owners were Taylor & Cameron, a Liverpool-based company, and the *Wallachia* was initially used by them on their Black Sea run. In 1893 she was sold to William Burrell & Son of Glasgow and soon started plying Burrell's well worn passage from Glasgow to the West Indies. Sir William Burrell (1861–1958) was a wealthy Glasgow shipowner with a lifelong passion for collecting art.

William Burrell first entered the family shipping firm Burrell & Son in 1876 at the tender age of 15. On his father's death in 1885 he and his elder brother George took over the management of the firm. Under their shrewd management the firm reached a position of international standing in worldwide tramping. A bold and effective yet simple formula led to immense commercial success. In a period of depression the brothers would order a large number of steamships at rock-bottom prices. They gambled that by the time the ships were ready to be launched the recession would be coming to an end. They could then win business easily with ships readily available to meet growing demand as the economy surged. At the same time they would be able to undercut their competitors. After several years of boom trading they would then sell their fleet when the market was at a high and then simply tick over until the next recession when the cycle could be repeated. In 1893–4 twelve ships were built and the ten-year-old *Wallachia* purchased. A few years later the entire fleet was sold at great profit. In 1905 they ordered 20 new steamers and then eight more in 1909/10. The outbreak of World War I saw dramatic rises in the market values of ships and between 1913 and 1916 they sold practically the entire fleet again. With his share of the proceeds William Burrell then devoted his life to his all-consuming passion: amassing a vast art collection. In 1944 the Burrell Collection was gifted to the City of Glasgow by Sir William and Lady Burrell and is now housed in a fine gallery at Pollok Park. It is one of the most varied and important collections in the UK.

After two years plying William Burrell & Sons' West Indies passage, in September 1895, the *Wallachia* was scheduled for another routine voyage from Glasgow to Trinidad and Demerara. The *Wallachia* lay berthed at the Queen's Dock, Glasgow as her holds were filled with her valuable cargo of coal, gin, whisky, beer, building materials, books, stationery, glassware and earthenware and other general goods destined to ease the rigours of life in the West Indies. Her deck cargo included stannous chloride (for use in the sugar industry) in two-gallon earthenware jars. By the morning of Sunday 29 September 1895 loading had been completed and Captain Walton made ready the vessel to leave the Queen's Dock on a journey that would take several weeks across the stormy Atlantic.

Opposite: Location chart of the wrecks *Wallachia* and *Akka*

S.S. WALLACHIA

No.1 Hold   No.2 Hold   No.3 Hold   No.4 Hold

By ten a.m. she had a head of steam, her mooring lines were cast off and she slipped out of the Queen's Dock. Her crew of 21 busily settled down to their well established shipboard routine as the *Wallachia* left her berth. The one solitary passenger aboard for the passage would have watched the crew busying themselves and perhaps looked longingly as Glasgow faded into the distance, wondering when he would ever see Scotland again.

General arrangement of the SS *Wallachia*

Sea conditions were poor. A heavy fog, common in autumn, hung in the air, making navigation dangerous and a test of seamanship. Two hours into the journey, at noon, the *Wallachia* was off the Tail of the Bank, nearing Greenock. Here the fog was so thick that she had to halt her journey and wait for an improvement in the sea conditions. The conditions improved in the early afternoon as the fog lifted slightly. Captain Walton put his engines ahead and the *Wallachia* got underway again, slowly passing down the river heading for the open water of the Firth of Clyde. As she passed the Cloch lighthouse on her southerly port beam, the fog thickened once again. Captain Walton took the *Wallachia* across the main channel towards the Argyll shore which he followed southwards down the Cowal Peninsula, keeping the land in sight in the poor conditions. Just before four p.m. the *Wallachia* entered a thicker bank of fog and, in the difficult conditions and poor visibility, grounded on a shoal off Innellan Pier, near the southmost point of the Cowal Peninsula. Thankfully the tide was rising and she quickly refloated and was able to continue with her journey southwards down the river.

That was the last piece of luck the *Wallachia* would have, for at about 4.10 pm disaster struck. Captain Walton, who had been carefully guiding his vessel down the river in these treacherous conditions, had successfully navigated the *Wallachia* to a point about a mile east of Toward Point with its distinctive and prominent lighthouse. Suddenly a large steamship materialised out of the fog, bearing down hard on his starboard bow. The poor visibility meant that the steamer was only seen at the last moment and Captain Walton had no time to take avoiding action. He was only able to order all hands clear of the fo'c'sle before the two vessels collided. The oncoming bows of the 1,406-ton Norwegian steamship *Flos* rammed into the starboard side of the *Wallachia*, ten feet back from the bows, slicing open the iron hull as though it were cardboard. A huge gash in the hull of the *Wallachia* appeared instantly and tons of cold, dark water started flooding into her hull. The two vessels were locked together in a fatal embrace as the full realisation of the calamity dawned on the crews of both vessels.

The captain of the *Flos*, alive to the situation, kept his engines ahead, helping to keep the two vessels locked together. This would slow the flood of water into the *Wallachia* and also give the bow support. The order to abandon the *Wallachia* was given and her four lifeboats were readied to be lowered from their davits down to the water below. The first lifeboat capsized as it was lowered but the crew of 22 and the sole passenger managed to safely lower and board two of the three remaining lifeboats and row clear of the vessel. Toward lighthouse was still visible to the north-west and the crew were able to row towards the shore and safety.

The captain of the *Flos* decided to attempt to take the *Wallachia* in tow to shallower water where she could be grounded and the ship and her valuable cargo saved. The engines of the *Flos* were put astern but as she backed away the gap in the *Wallachia*'s hull that she had effectively been plugging was opened up to the sea and the rate of flow of water into the *Wallachia* increased dramatically. She immediately began to settle by the bow and the attempt to take her in tow was abandoned.

At about 4.35 p.m., some 25 minutes after the fateful ramming, the *Wallachia* went down by the bow, slipping under the dark waters of the Clyde. As she went under tons of cold water made contact with her boilers, causing a large explosion. As she passed from sight the waters of the Clyde frothed and boiled as air was forced from her hull by the pressure of the water rushing into her.

Although the *Wallachia* settled on an even keel in deep water of 34 metres, her masts rose to just one metre short of the surface and were an obvious danger to navigation in the estuary. As a result, just twelve days later, on 11 October 1895 the salvage vessel *Torch*, owned by the Clyde Lighthouse Trustees, appeared at the scene of the sinking and anchored over the wreck. A hard-hat diver was sent down to inspect the wreck and reported that the vessel was lying upright in 20 fathoms of water. Her two large tubular steel masts were then blasted off. The *Wallachia* was thereafter left to lie peacefully in her watery grave and the memory of the once proud ship faded with the passing of the years. The last official trace of her was as a wreck symbol on an Admiralty chart of 1905. From then on she was forgotten about and passed into oblivion, just another statistic destined to haunt the pages of old record books.

For more than 80 years the *Wallachia* lay slowly rusting and decaying on the seabed, known only by local fishermen as an underwater obstruction. Any human memory of the cause of their snagged lines and nets had long gone. The first trace of her in modern times came in December 1976 when an unknown wreck was located by HMS *Sheraton* using sonar. Three divers were sent down to investigate but were unable to identify the mystery wreck. At that time it was noted that the iron propeller was still in place on the wreck. In March 1977 navy divers went down on the wreck again and were able to glean some more information about her. It was found that she was holed on her starboard side and that this was most probably the cause of her sinking.

In October 1977 the *Wallachia* was discovered for sport divers by members of the Girvan branch of the Scottish Sub Aqua Club. They had been alerted to the presence of a large underwater obstruction by local fishermen who had given them the Decca co-ordinates. On the same weekend that they received the information they were able to go out and investigate the site. After a few passes over the site a large object was picked up on the echo-sounder. Now the hunt was really on.

Their initial exploratory dives confirmed that the obstruction was a large steel or iron-hulled steamship but her identity could not be established. Research through the following winter proved fruitless in identifying her. The National Maritime Museum, HM Customs & Excise, and Admiralty Hydrographic Department, the Public Records Office, Southampton Chamber of Commerce, Southampton Public Library, the *Glasgow Herald*, the Nautical College and many other possible sources were checked but from none of these could any clue to the identity of the mystery vessel be found. There were no readily accessible records which could point them in the right direction and reveal the identity of the mystery wreck. The *Wallachia* would hold her secret until the following summer when, in August 1978, the breakthrough came that would throw off the shroud of mystery. After a succession of exploratory dives on the wreck by the club the builder's plate was located. Although it did not have the actual vessel's name on it, it did have the builder's name and the yard number:

OSWALD MORDAUNT & CO.

SHIPBUILDERS & ENGINEERS

SOUTHAMPTON

SHIP No. 202 1883

From this specific information the club were able to conclusively establish the unknown wreck's identity as the *Wallachia* by the middle of 1979. The Hydrographic Department of the MoD, acting on information from the club, asked HMS *Sheraton*, then surveying the Clyde, to investigate the wreck and check the findings of the club. Using sonar, echo-soundings and inspections by teams of divers HMS *Sheraton* was able to confirm the club's information and the wreck, which had vanished from the Admiralty charts in 1905, once again became marked on the charts after a gap of nearly 80 years. One of the Clyde's best kept secrets had finally been revealed.

The wreck of the once proud *Wallachia* is now justly acclaimed as one of the most important of the many Clyde shipwrecks. She lies about one mile to the east of Toward Point on the Cowal Peninsula not far from the main shipping channel in 34 metres of water. Since she was rediscovered in 1977 by sport divers her popularity as one of the Clyde's best wreck dives has increased steadily. When the first divers found her she had lain untouched on the seabed for nearly 80 years. No one had salvaged her. Everything was there on her, just as it was the day she went down in 1895. She was every diver's dream; a virgin wreck, a time capsule from the last century. Word of the find soon leaked out and the lure of diving on such a fascinating wreck drew divers in increasing numbers to her. She is now a focus for Clyde diving and most weekends there will be a number of dive boats out on site, lining up their transits and then locating her with an echo-sounder.

Toward Point is a notorious promontory that, despite a distinctive lighthouse, has become a graveyard for a number of vessels over the centuries. The 190-foot, iron paddle-steamer *Lady Gertrude* came to grief here in 1877, running aground with no loss of life. Despite attempts to haul her off by tugs she broke her back and became a total loss. In 1889, just four years before the *Wallachia* would founder here, the 187-foot steamship *Ovington*, stationary and preparing to anchor because of bad weather that had made navigation hazardous, was rammed by the 1,500-ton steamer *Queen Victoria* which, in the poor visibility, had mistaken her lights for the Skelmorlie Buoy. A huge hole was torn in her port side between the bridge and bow. Most of the crew were able to scramble across on to the bow of the *Queen Victoria* whilst the two ships were locked together but within five minutes of the collision she had gone down by the bow in 35 metres of water one mile south of Toward Lighthouse. In 1940 the 105-foot auxiliary steamer *Penola* collided with another vessel here and sank just west of Toward lighthouse. The *Wallachia* has much company in the depths here.

The *Wallachia* herself is some 259 feet in length and so in any one dive it is quite possible to circumnavigate the wreck and quickly get an idea of her layout. The only impediment to that will be the notorious Clyde visibility – or, more realistically, the lack of it. Unlike the *Akka*, where the wreck lies in shallower, lighter and clearer water, the *Wallachia* lies in an area where unfortunately it is all too common to get visibility of only a few metres. This, added to the depth and general darkness down

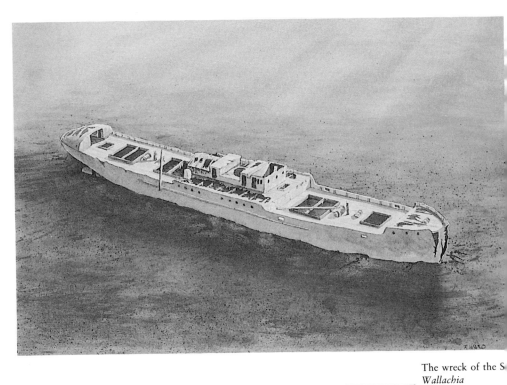

The wreck of the S
Wallachia

WALLACHIA
STEAMER 1734 gross tons

starboard

port

30 m

34 m

on the wreck, can make for an uncomfortable dive for those not accustomed to this form of diving. Do not let that put you off diving her, however. She is a great wreck dive and should certainly not be missed.

The poor visibility will become apparent as soon as you roll over the side of the dive boat into the water. On a good day the visibility will be two or three metres at the surface, something akin to diving in a whisky bottle. The particles in suspension that are carried down from the upper reaches of the river close the visibility down completely. This high concentration of particles in suspension manifests itself in force as divers descend down the shotline. The available natural light penetrating down from the surface is quickly filtered out. By about ten metres down it is very dark and gloomy with most divers switching on their torches for a glimpse of the shotline they are following down. By 20 metres down it is, quite simply, completely black. Your eyes will not yet have adjusted to night vision and so, other than the shotline you are clinging to in the beam of your torch, you will not be able to make anything out at all. For the inexperienced diver this can be quite a disconcerting feeling. The *Wallachia* is one of those wrecks that most British wreck divers are familiar with – the sort that you bang into before you actually see it!

Visibility down on the wreck itself appears much better than in the shallower surface levels although even the most experienced Clyde wreck diver can have a little difficulty initially in the blackness working out exactly where they are on the wreck. A good, strong torch is essential as diving the *Wallachia* is, for all practical purposes, a night dive. Pencil

The ship's bell recovered from the *Wallachia*

torches and the like are a waste of time on this wreck and a good night-diving torch is essential. All the serious Clyde wreck divers carry the biggest torches money can buy and once on your way down to the wreck you can see why. Like a lot of Clyde diving, the currents on this wreck can be unpredictable. Often when the tide is running on the surface it is slack at depth and vice versa.

If you have never dived the *Wallachia* before you will find your first dive on her exhilarating. There is so much of interest that simply trying to grasp this once proud lady of the seas will be a challenge in itself. Every dive you subsequently make on the *Wallachia* will reveal something new and of interest. If the visibility is good she is a fascinating wreck, so reminiscent of the majestic era of steam that bred her – and eventually consigned her to her grave in the Clyde.

The wreck of the *Wallachia* sits on an even keel in 34 metres of water

Part of the SS *Wallachia*'s famous cargo of McEwan's beer and stout bottles with (below) the corks still bearing the maker's familiar name

Porthole recovered
from the SS
Wallachia

at Latitude 55 51 40.0 N and Longitude 04 57 07.0 W. She is quite heavily
settled into the muddy seabed and there is no noticeable scour at either
side of the wreck. Although in her heyday she had a draught of 18 feet
(approximately five metres), the highest point of the wreck today stands
only about nine metres clear of the seabed at 25 metres. The average
depth found at deck level is about 30 metres.

The wreck has proved to be an unending source of interesting artefacts.
Her three foredeck holds are quite heavily filled with silt that billows up
in huge clouds as the downdraught from the diver's fin strokes hits it. A
series of mini explosions of silt follow the diver around as he explores
the hold. The ship's brass bell was recovered soon after her initial
discovery, the inscription 'Wallachia 1883' still easily legible on it. The
ship's steering wheel was recovered in pristine condition still on its column.
Eight spokes radiated out from its centre which had a striking brass wheel
plate on it with the ship's name etched on it. Many other smaller artefacts
from the *Wallachia* have seen the light of day once again after an
immersion of more than 80 years in the murky waters of the Clyde.

The *Wallachia* rests close to the Wemyss Bay-to-Rothesay ferry route
and the shipping channel on the west of the Clyde. As a result, good boat
cover is a prerequisite for this dive and an A-flag (the signal to other
vessels that divers are down) should be flown prominently. The most
convenient boat access for RIBs is the RNLI slip at Largs waterfront.
From here you will have a journey of some 20 minutes out to the site.

The bows of the *Wallachia* point roughly towards the north. The lines
of the bow itself point straight down into the darkness towards the seabed
in the classic vertical rake of the day. At the starboard side of the bow
there is a gaping gash, the fatal damage from the collision with the *Flos*
that sent her to her doom. It was through this breach in her hull that tons
of seawater flooded after the *Flos* reversed away, sending her down bow

Binoculars recovered
from the SS
Wallachia

first. Portholes line the sides of the hull here where they once illuminated
the raised fo'c'sle. Two rear-facing bulkhead doors are set in the fo'c'sle here
at main deck level, allowing divers with care to enter and exit. On top of
the fo'c'sle sits a large winch and old fishing nets are snagged here and there.

Moving astern from the bow the first of the three foredeck holds is
found. Each of the holds is well filled with silt but a lot of rummaging
around in the silt here over the years has revealed some items of real
interest. Hold No 1 is set by itself just aft of the raised fo'c'sle at the bow.
Between it and hold No 2, further aft, originally stood the large tubular
steel foremast. This mast, along with the mainmast towards the stern,
was removed by divers from the salvage vessel *Torch* in 1895 to clear the
danger for passing sea traffic. Its stump can still be made out between the
holds, flanked forward and aft by large deck winches which would have
operated a derrick system for loading and unloading the cargo. A section
of the foremast – or, more probably, a derrick from it – now lies fore
and aft across holds Nos 2 and 3 just in front of the raised bridge deck.
This mast quite often hooks the dive boat's grapple and is a good orienting
feature to help you work out where on the wreck you are when you first
go down on it. Standing here on the deck at a depth of about 30 metres,
it is pitch dark, the surface far above out of sight. Little light filters down
through the murky layers of the Clyde to the wreck here. It is difficult to
imagine that when she first sank her mast rose up to just one metre short
of the surface.

The famous two-gallon stannous chloride jars still bear the maker's name on their lids

The hatches to hold Nos 2 and 3 are set close together in front of the bridge superstructure. Rummaging around in them, dark beer bottles and clear spirit bottles can be found amongst the silt. Some of the bottles in this hold have become concreted together and are now inseparable. This is only a foretaste of the vast numbers that await discovery in the aft holds.

Moving further aft a raised bulkhead blocks your path. Originally, at either side of the deck here, steps would have allowed the crew access to the deck above where the bridge itself is situated. This superstructure contains the cabins, galley, bathroom and coal bunkers and at either side of the hull there is a row of portholes that would have allowed fresh air and light into these areas. The wooden decking above has rotted away, giving easy access into these rooms. Beneath this deck level was the boiler-room, set forward of the engine-room and funnel.

The bridge itself is set on top of this superstructure deck and has forward-looking portholes and entry doors from its port and starboard decks. The roof has rotted away, leaving it completely open above. The captain's quarters were originally situated in the raised bridge deck, just aft of the bridge itself. The quarters are entered by two doors, one at either side. Here, immediately behind the bridge and captain's quarters, the large single funnel was originally situated. The funnel has long since rotted away and collapsed to leave a cavernous black hole about six feet wide and down which two divers can easily descend simultaneously to explore the engine-room below on two deck levels. Landing on the deck below, the divers can look aft into the engine-room through a wide opening. The most striking feature here is the large circular top of a piston-head some five feet across with its rod rising up from its centre. At either side of this, engine-room catwalks can be made out. Divers can, with care, pass below decks at either side of the piston-head and fin along inside the engine-room to exit through the distinctive skylights of the engine-room's pitched roof, aft of the funnel opening. Alternatively these skylights can be used as the entry point to get into the engine-room below decks.

At either side of the engine-room on the raised deck there was a solitary raised companionway doorway, facing aft to allow the crew immediate access to the accommodation and engine-room. The starboard doorway structure is still *in situ* but only part of the port side doorway remains. Here on the port side a solitary lifeboat davit reveals where the lifeboats that saved the crew's life as she sank were once located.

At the aftmost bulkhead of the engine-room superstructure there is a drop down once again to main deck level. Just aft of the engine-room are the remains of the deck cargo of two-gallon stannous chloride earthenware jars. Only fragments of these now remain.

Set in the wooden planked deck here are three more holds. Finning over the edge of the two open holds, there is no great drop down into them. These holds are full to a few feet from the top with large dark beer bottles and smaller stout bottles. As you drop into the hold all you see is the top of a huge mound of beer bottles with scores of bottles sticking up through the heavy layer of silt that has settled in the hold over the years. Nearly all these bottles still hold their 100-year-old beer and have their corks in place.

In between hold Nos 4 and 5 can be found the stump of the mainmast with two powerful deck winches set forward and aft of the mast to work its derrick system. Although the tubular mainmast was removed in 1895, a section of it or possibly a derrick lies on the deck, sticking out over the starboard side of the hull. An open hatch allows access down a fixed ladder into the covered aftmost hold which is deeply filled by silt. At the stern is another raised section of accommodation superstructure, housing the emergency steering gear, a toilet and a store. Doorways allow divers to peer inside and follow the beams of their torches as they sweep around, momentarily bringing light to this otherwise black void. Part of the roofing over this area has rotted away, exposing the structural ribs of the deck-house. The stern itself still displays its fine, rounded lines and sweeps down and inwards in an overhang towards the rudder, now well embedded in the silty seabed.

The *Wallachia* is a classic Scottish wreck dive. Like most wrecks there is good fish life on the wreck, attracted by the safety of its intricate nooks and crannies and the abundance of rich pickings on it. The wreck itself appears grey/brown in the diver's torch beam as a result of the heavy covering of sediment swept down on to it over the years. Wherever there is a foothold, sponges and anemones have colonised the area. Their bright colours illuminated by the torch beams are a vivid contrast to the dull blandness of the silty wreck itself.

When divers first reach the wreck after their descent from the surface, their eyes are still attuned for the bright topside light levels and unable to discern much at all other than the parts lit up by their torches. The diver seems suspended in a black, inky, impenetrable void with only the beam of his torch to light up a small area of the wreck. As is common with night diving, however, after ten or 20 minutes down on the wreck a diver's night vision starts to take over. Halfway through a dive on the *Wallachia* a diver will be able to make out the silhouettes of large sections of the wreck and its superstructure. What initially seemed pitch black now appears perceptibly lighter. The water above appears to have a greenish hue to it and it is this contrast that allows divers to make out silhouettes of the bridge and superstructure.

The currents in this are are unpredictable and divers should ensure that they know exactly where their grapple is hooked on to the wreck to return to it at the end of the dive before ascending. The wreck is small enough for this to be easily and safely accomplished. Just drifting off the wreck and ascending should not be encouraged. The current will sweep divers quite some distance away from the wreck and their surface boat cover before they break the surface. If the boat cover has lost track of the bubble stream in choppy seas then they may be unaware of the extent of the current and not looking in the right area for the divers to ascend. The wreck is near to very busy shipping lanes and divers drifting, separated from their dive boat in these waters can cause much confusion and annoyance for vessels plying these waters, apart from the obvious danger to the divers themselves. There are many stories of divers being swept away from the wreck and being recovered miles downstream by other vessels seeing them in distress in the water. As a general rule, divers on this wreck should ensure that they can find their way back to the line to ascend.

Essential Information

Boat launch site: For RIBS the slip at the RNLI station on Largs waterfront.
Tidal conditions: 0–1 knot.
Visibility: 1–10 metres. Average 3 metres.
Maximum depth: Seabed 34 metres. Deck 30 metres. Least depth 25 metres.
Coastguard: (0475) 29988 or (051) 931 3341.
Police: Inverkip (0475) 521222. Skelmorlie (0475) 520121.
Air supplies: Kip Watersports, Kip Marina (0475) 521281. C & C Marine Services, Largs Yacht Haven (0475) 687180.
Hydrographic chart: Little Cumbrae Island to Cloch Point No 1907.
Sea area: Malin.
Recompression chambers: Western Infirmary, Glasgow (041) 339 8822. HMS *Neptune*, Faslane, Helensburgh (0436) 4321. Millport Marine Laboratory (0475) 553 581.
Position: Lat 55 51 41 N, Long 04 57 07 W.

For more information on the many and varied Clyde shipwrecks, *Clyde Shipwrecks* by Peter Moir and Ian Crawford, published by Moir Crawford, 1988, is highly recommended.

THE *AKKA*
Firth of Clyde

The mighty wreck of the Swedish steel motor vessel *Akka* is the largest divable wreck in the Firth of Clyde today. A combination of factors place her high on the list of Scotland's greatest wrecks. The wreck is still largely intact and it is possible for the visiting diver to swim along corridors with cabins leading off and drift from one deck to another up and down companionways. Lying in a barren mud desert, the *Akka* has become an artificial reef and a profusion of sealife awaits the diver. She is literally covered in dead men's fingers and a blaze of orange and white plumrose anemones. Large shoals of fish school around her, living off the wreck and, at the same time, finding safe refuge in her deepest recesses when danger threatens. Seals can often be seen on the surface and cannot resist coming in close for a better look at the divers, these strange, noisy intruders in their underwater world. The *Akka* has it all.

The *Akka* was built in Gothenberg, Sweden by A/B Götaverken and completed in July 1942. She was registered in Stockholm and owned by Trafikaktieb Grängesberg Oxelösund. She measured 442 feet ten inches in length with a beam of 56 feet nine inches and a draught of 25 feet ten and three-quarter inches. She had one steel-plated main deck and a shelter deck beneath. Two SA six-cylinder (680 × 1500 mm) oil engines built by the shipbuilders themselves provided her power. Her boilers developed 85 lbs of pressure, enough to achieve speeds of 12.5 knots. She had a gross weight of 5,409 tons and a net weight of 3,053 tons.

Apart from her engine-rooms amidships and the storerooms and accommodation at her stern and bow, most of her length below decks was taken up by six cavernous cargo holds. Eight hatches gave access to these holds for loading and unloading. All of these hatches were 26 feet wide but varied in length from $13\frac{1}{2}$ feet to 28 feet.

At her very stern was an accommodation deck-house holding the crew's cabins. Above this was situated the crew's bar and at either side of this superimposed deck-house a lifeboat hung in its davit. Beneath the main deck at shelter deck level were messes, stores and toilets ringed by a row of portholes. Forward of this deck-house stood two derricks with gibs protruding from them over hold No 6.

Her main superstructure was situated amidships above her engine-rooms. At shelter deck level were located the hospital room, crew's mess rooms, galley (at the very rear of this area), pantry and toilets. Also located here, conveniently close to the engine-rooms below, were the first and second engineers' and the chief eingineer's cabin quarters.

On the main deck above, a flight of steps at either side of the hull led up to the promenade deck. The lounge and saloon were housed inside this first level of superstructure at the very front. At either side of the motor casing through which the funnel rose were a line of officers' cabins, bathrooms, the pilot's cabin and linen rooms. Her mainmast rose out from the rear of this superstructure through the promenade deck itself, flanked on either side by a tall derrick.

Another two flights of steps led up from the promenade deck to the boat deck. A further two lifeboats swung in davits here, one at either side of the funnel. Forward of the funnel and looking out over the foredeck to the bow were the captain's dayroom, bedroom and toilet. Immediately above this deck level and conveniently placed right above the captain's accommodation was the navigating bridge deck which housed the wheel-house and radio room.

A further pair of derricks was set forward of the bridge between hold Nos 3 and 4. Her foremast was located near the bow between hold Nos 1 and 2 with two further derricks at either side. At her very bow in her fo'c'sle were storerooms and at shelter deck level below her chain lockers.

The *Akka* was a well-designed and efficient cargo vessel and served her owners well for 14 years before her seadays came to an untimely and tragic end in the Firth of Clyde. On Wednesday 4 April 1956 she cast off her mooring ropes at her home port of Oxelösund on Sweden's eastern coast on the Baltic Sea on what was to be her final voyage. Her holds were filled with a cargo of iron ore bound for Glasgow. She slipped out of port into the Baltic Sea and headed southwards. Soon she was rounding the southernmost tip of Sweden and following the coast as it turned northwards. The *Akka* then entered the *Kattegat*, the narrow strip of sea between the east coast of Denmark and Sweden's west coast, the only channel in and out of the Baltic Sea. After rounding the northernmost tip of Denmark she passed into the *Skagerrak*, the scene of the famous Battle of Jutland during World War I. Here the mighty German High Seas Fleet and the British Grand Fleet had clashed in the only major confrontation of the two fleets during the war. In eleven hours of battle in these waters the British Grand Fleet lost three battle cruisers, three cruisers, one light cruiser and seven destroyers. More than six thousand British servicemen were killed in action with 510 wounded and 177 taken prisoner by the Germans. Passing on into the open expanses of the North Sea, the *Akka* ploughed on along her well-worn route to Scotland's bustling industrial port. The voyage across the North Sea past the Orkney islands off northern Scotland and down the west coast of Scotland towards the Firth of Clyde was uneventful. The crew soon fell into the regular pattern of daily life aboard ship.

The MV *Akka*, lightly laden

After five days at sea, on Monday 9 April, the *Akka* rounded the Mull of Kintyre and, passing the dark, rocky cliffs of the island of Ailsa Craig, entered the Firth of Clyde. Journey's end was close at hand and the crew's spirits were lifted at the thought of some time ashore. She continued up the Firth, passing the Isle of Arran to the north on her port side. At 8.15 p.m. she passed Small Cumbrae light and by nine p.m. that evening she was abeam of the Cumbrae islands. Pressing on further up the Firth at ten knots, the majestic Isle of Bute slipped by on her port beam. Soon on a radar course of 009 degrees, she was approaching Innellan where the Firth narrows considerably. At 9.22 p.m. her master, Captain Sundin, rang down on the ship's telegraph to the engine-room for half speed. The *Akka* slowed and made ready to take the pilot aboard who would guide her in her final approach to her berth further up the River Clyde. He could see the light on the treacherous Gantock Rocks to port some distance ahead and to starboard, the Cloch Point lighthouse. The captain and pilot would steer the *Akka* well clear of the Gantocks. They are a dangerous clump of rocks that rise up from a depth of 20 to 24 metres to break the surface about a mile south-east of Dunoon. They are a well-known hazard to navigation in the Clyde and have claimed many vessels over the years. A small tower with an unmanned light had been built on the Rocks to warn mariners of their presence.

At this point the *Akka* was now only hours away from docking at the end of an uneventful voyage. Captain Sundin ordered a course change to 056 degrees (radar) and it was immediately noticed that the *Akka* responded very slowly to her rudder. The captain knew they were in treacherous waters and so, at 9.26 p.m., unable to steer his ship away from her course bearing down on the Rocks he ordered her engines

stopped, although by now she had picked up her course of 056 degrees. Master and crew held their breaths as the drama unfolded. The forward momentum of the 5,409 tons of the *Akka* was considerable and she was too close to the Rocks to slow in time. The *Akka* was therefore carried on to the Gantocks, driven on by her momentum. Many folk ashore in Dunoon and Gourock reported hearing the tearing and grinding as her hull was rent open to the sea. The quiet stillness of the evening was shattered by the sounds of the ship's torture, carried over the waves by the gentle evening breeze. People rushed out from their homes to see what was happening and were able to look on helplessly at the *Akka*'s death throes.

The MV *Akka* in her wartime colours (National Maritime Museum, Greenwich)

Deep in the *Hispania*'s engine-room, a diver examines the crownhead valve

A diver, facing towards the bow, examines the marine life on the walkway in front of the *Hispania*'s bridge. The starboard side ventilator funnel can be seen in the rear

The roof of the *Hispania*'s stern accommodation deck-house has rotted away, allowing safe and easy access

At the very stern of the *Hispania* the turning windlass for the emergency steering gear still stands in place

Forward from the *Hispania*'s stern accommodation deck-house, the top of the spare propeller juts out of its small storage hold

The ever-increasing list of the *Hispania* is evident as a diver passes along the companionway running along the port side of the bridge superstructure

The hull of the *San Tiburcio* is covered in a rich carpet of sea life

The plating along the front bulkhead of the *San Tiburcio*'s stern accommodation deck-house has rotted away to leave a skeleton of struts and spars

The topmost blade of the *Hispania*'s spare propeller rears out of its storage
hold just forward of the stern accommodation deck-house

Divers examine the winch between the *Fram*'s two stern holds at a depth of 46
metres

Centre plate from the wheel of the *Wallachia*

One of the finds from the *Wallachia*

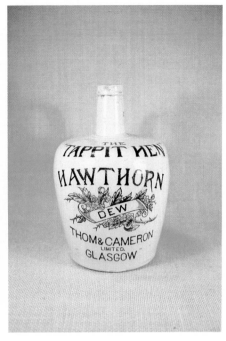

The *Rondo*'s rudder stands nearly vertically at the shallowest part of the wreck. The prop shaft can be seen at bottom right

The mainmast A-frame on the *Rondo* at 25 metres

The floor of the *Hispania*'s engine-room is a tangled mass of twisted pipes, cables, machinery and catwalks

Porthole recovered from the *Akka*

The Gantock Rocks had effortlessly torn her hull open along almost half her length from hold No 2 and tons of seawater were flooding into the stricken vessel. Captain Sundin, reacting speedily to the *Akka*'s predicament, rang down to the engine-room on the ship's telegraph for the engines to be put into reverse in an attempt to get his ship into shallower water so that she could be saved. Unfortunately by doing this he increased the rate of flow of water into the holds and engine-room. Realising that the ship was lost and that she was sinking quickly, he then ordered all engines stopped and gave the order to abandon ship. Lifeboats were lowered over the side of the *Akka* as she quickly developed a list to port.

Within a period of only three or four minutes from running aground on the Rocks the *Akka* heeled over on to her port side and settled quickly into the waters of the Clyde. As she sank blasts of steam shot water spouts high into the air and as the cold seawater flooding into her made contact with her boilers there was a large explosion. The *Akka* went down so quickly that the lifeboats did not have time to clear the area and the suction and surface turmoil created by her passing and the waves from the explosion sunk a number of them. Their unfortunate occupants who only minutes before were in sight of their destination and looking forward to a few days ashore were pitched into freezing cold water, capable of shocking and numbing a man within minutes. Thankfully the sinking was relatively close to shore and had been witnessed by a number of townsfolk who had summoned help. Within a few minutes a number of rescue vessels arrived at the scene of the sinking including the ferry *Granny Kempock* and the aptly named pilot cutter *Gantock*. They were able to pluck most of the crew from the freezing waters in time. Sadly, three of the crew went down with the ship and three more died on their way to hospital. There were 27 survivors.

When dawn came the following morning, the daylight revealed the topmost 12 feet of the *Akka*'s two masts sticking out of the water, marking her site. After she struck the Gantocks and tried to reverse off, she had been carried further up the river before she had sunk. She came to rest on an even keel on the western edge of the Dunoon Bank, a shallow bank of rock and mud to the north-east of the Gantock Rocks. The Dunoon Bank rises up from a general depth of 70 to 100 metres to just 30 to 40 metres from the surface where the *Akka* had finally sunk.

The wreck of the *Akka* was quickly marked by a light buoy to warn vessels of her presence whilst the owners and insurers began discussing the possibility of salvaging the wreck and her cargo. The negotiations, however, dragged on unresolved until three months later when a passing fishing vessel hit the wreck. This prompted urgent clearance work and in September 1956 salvage and dispersal operations took place. Clearance divers from Metal Industries using explosives were able to remove the top two levels of her bridge along with her funnel and masts.

The official Swedish inquiry into the sinking found three main causes for the disaster. Firstly, it was accepted that there may have been a technical fault in the steering mechanism. Secondly, Captain Sundin was found to be at fault for relying on radar bearings and distances on a night with good visual conditions. Thirdly, Captain Sundin was held to have underestimated the time for a change in course to take effect when the vessel was fully laden.

In 1962 a two-boat drag sweep reported the site clear at 46 feet with a foul reported at 47 feet. In 1963 the wreck was marked by a green conical light buoy and in 1966 she was surveyed by divers from HMS *Vidal*. They reported that she was sitting nearly upright in a depth of 90 to 140 feet on a bottom of sand, mud, stones and shell with no noticeable scour. They found that there was no obstruction shallower than 50 feet. The bows were noted to be pointing southwards and not northwards as had been previously thought and she was sitting on a line bearing 155/335 degrees. The least depth over her bows was noted to be 51 feet, her bridge, 50 feet and her poop deck 60 feet.

More recent surveys have reported separate wreckage lying to the west of the wreck itself. This is probably the superstructure that would have been dumped here after the salvage operations in 1956.

Once the wreck had been made safe for smaller vessels to pass over her by the salvage operations, she was left to rest in peace. Lying on the shallow Dunoon Banks outside the shipping lanes she was not a hazard to larger vessels who would not be passing over the Banks. Total dispersal of the wreck therefore was not justified. The wreck of the once proud *Akka* was then ignored and subsequently forgotten about until the recent boom in sport diving when she was rediscovered in all her glory. The years on the seabed had transformed the *Akka* into an underwater reef, populated by countless species of sea creatures. She had become one of Scotland's greatest wrecks.

Today the wreck of the mighty *Akka* lies on an even keel at Latitude 55 56 43.0 N and Longitude 04 54 20.0 W on the north-west side of the Dunoon Bank. She lies on a sloping muddy bottom facing down the river, to the south. Her bow is in about 30 metres of water and her stern in about 40 metres. Her location is easily and conveniently fixed by the large port hand yellow cardinal navigation buoy that marks the main shipping lane. The *Akka*'s stern lies about 50 metres north-east of the buoy and she points south to south-east down the river. The least depths down to the deck are about 16 metres at the shallower bow and 24 metres at the deeper stern.

Despite the heavy traffic in the Clyde there are surprisingly few good slips at which to launch your RIB. The slip at the RNLI boathouse on Largs waterfront, also recommended for the *Wallachia*, is about the best. This is a good slip in a sheltered location and can be used at all states of the tide to launch and retrieve even the largest and heaviest RIB. Do not obstruct the slip or the car parking bays which are for RNLI personnel

The wreck of the
MV *Akka*

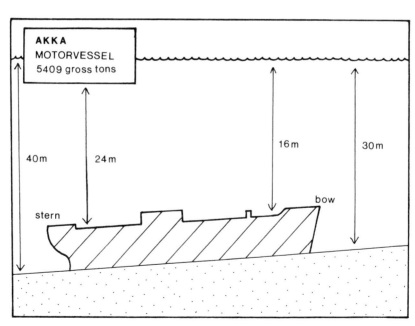

only. The trip from Largs to the wreck site will take about 30 minutes. There is a good sheltered slip in Cardwell Bay, Gourock opposite Adams Boat Yard. For a great day's diving try launching at Largs, diving the *Wallachia* in the morning and then calling into Kip Marina before diving the *Akka* in the afternoon. Kip Watersports dive shop is close to the pontoons in the Marina and it's not too much of a hike to carry your bottles there for charging. Whilst getting your bottles filled you can then stroll up to the restaurant and bar facility overlooking the Marina and enjoy the food and drink served there. There is an outdoor wet area where you can drip dry whilst charging up your own internal batteries. Once rested and with freshly filled bottles you can head over to the *Akka* for the afternoon's dive before heading back down the Firth to Largs again. The closest launching site for your RIB is at Dunoon itself on the Cowal, north-westerly side of the Firth. From here it is only a short trip of ten minutes out to the wreck site. To get to Dunoon, however, would entail a long road journey or a ferry trip from Gourock if you were coming from central Scotland. If you were spending time on Cowal diving other sites then Dunoon would be your best launch site. There is a good slip in West Bay, Dunoon and an alternative at the Yacht Club, Holy Loch.

The River Clyde has for centuries been a heavily navigated stretch of water and this is more true now than ever before. Ships large and small will continually pass by the dive site, keeping a respectful distance whilst divers are down. It is not uncommon to have a black naval submarine pass you on the surface. It must be remembered that you are diving right at the very edge of the main shipping channel and that therefore it is absolutely essential that the 'divers are down' A-flag is flown to alert nearby vessels to your actions.

Once on site the wreck can easily be located with an echo-sounder, the large wreck itself and the clouds of fish that normally envelop it giving good, clear readings. There will be no mistaking the large trace that the awesome size of the *Akka* will produce on an otherwise flat, shelving bottom. Conveniently there is quite often a small plastic buoy already attached to the wreck. If there is no buoy then a grapple can be snagged on to the wreck.

Once moored on site you will easily be able to pick out the treacherous Gantock Rocks that caused the *Akka* to founder about half a mile off to your south-west. On top of the Rocks the white stone-built column with its navigation warning light on top can be made out. The town of Dunoon, a mile or two off to the west on the Cowal Peninsula, seems close, the buildings easily discernible.

Like all Clyde diving there is always the tidal current to bear in mind. To get the *Akka* at her best she should be dived, if possible, at high water slack on a neap tide when the visibility will be reasonably good. In mid-run the tidal current can reach two knots around the Dunoon Bank. If there is a bit of a current running then you will have to keep a good grip on the buoy line as you go down. It is not absolutely essential to get slack water as it is on the *Hispania* in the Sound of Mull. There, if you miss slack water you can easily find yourself in a three-knot current, hanging on to a deck rail in the prone position! The sides of the *Akka* rise quite high above the deck and give protection from the current once you are down on the wreck. If there is a current running, however, it will make it difficult to see a large section of the wreck and make it back to the buoy line to ascend at the end of your dive.

The wreck of the *Akka* has something to offer every diver. She is a big wreck, some 442 feet in length, and so will take several dives to become familiar with. It is possible to swim her length in one dive but difficult to return to the buoy line where you started. The depth limits your bottom time on her and because of the potential current in the river you will want to make sure that you get back to the buoy line to ascend. The last thing you want is to ascend away from the line and be carried away from the wreck in these busy waters. At every stage of her length there is something of interest: the raised fo'c'sle at the bow, the bridge and engine-room, the cavernous holds and the aft accommodation at the stern with its covered companionway passing right around it.

The wreck itself has been heavily colonised by orange and white plumrose anemones giving the wreck a rich, colourful appearance, much like the *Hispania*. A profusion of dead men's fingers, sponges and soft corals cling to handrails and rigging, producing blazes of brightness as the diver's torch sweeps over them. Being an artificial reef, the *Akka* has become home to large schools of fish which are able to feed on the smaller members of the food chain and, in turn, seek refuge from predators in the companionways and dark recesses of the wreck. With such a profusion of fish/food available it is not surprising that seals are often seen around the wreck. It is quite common to see seals on the surface as divers kit up in their dive boat. As always the seals' natural curiosity about these strange neoprene-clad invaders of their underwater realm overcomes any sense of danger that they might have at the divers' presence and it is quite common to have them swim in close for a good look. Some will even follow divers around on the wreck like faithful dogs.

Although much Clyde diving is in poor visibility it is quite common to get clear conditions on the *Akka*. The upper layers of the Clyde are often very silty and murky, blotting out the light and reducing visibility to a few feet. On the *Akka*, however, as divers descend through the upper surface layers the visibility improves and at depth it can be very clear but still quite dark. Unlike the *Wallachia*, which seems like a night dive even on the brightest summer's day, the *Akka* appears light but gloomy. It is shallower and the water appears clearer. As a result a lot more natural light is able to penetrate down to the wreck, giving average visibility of about five to ten metres as opposed to the two or three metres on the *Wallachia*. A good night-diving torch is still required to properly explore the *Akka* and investigate the cavernous holds and intriguing accommodation.

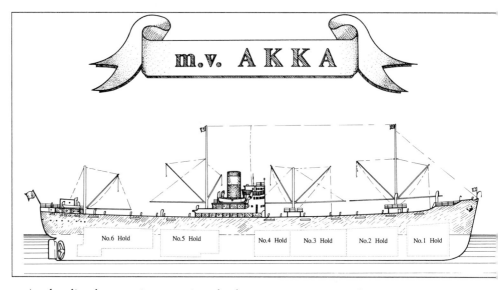

m.v. AKKA

No.6 Hold No.5 Hold No.4 Hold No.3 Hold No.2 Hold No.1 Hold

As the dive boat arrives on site, the boatman manoeuvres her into position above the wreck. Keeping a watchful eye on the echo-sounder, he approaches the buoy. The bottom shows uniformly flat at about 40 metres. Suddenly the bottom trace on the echo-sounder jumps up to 24 metres: they are over the stern. The dive marshal once again runs over the details for the dive, making sure that the divers are aware of the expected depths and permitted times down on the wreck. Each diver does a double check on his buddy diver's equipment, checking that his air supply is ready and that vital direct-feed hoses to his dry suit and buoyancy compensator jacket are connected. Once the checks are completed the divers are ready. They sit expectantly on the tubes of the dive boat and then roll over backwards into the water, disappearing in an explosion of bubbles. The splash rebounds upwards as the divers right themselves quickly and swim to the buoy line which will guide them down to the wreck. The *Akka* is far below, well out of sight. Without the rope to guide them as they descend the divers could well be swept away from the wreck by the current.

After a final OK signal to each other the descent to the wreck starts. The visibility in the upper layers is only about three metres on this dive and the divers have to descend slowly, keeping a close eye on the blurred figure of their companion close by. The loose dry suit is pressed against the body by the pressure and very soon a marked squeeze is felt on the body. The divers relieve the discomfort by bleeding some air into the suits via direct-feed hoses from the air cylinders on their backs. The increasing water pressure is also felt on the eardrums, the pressure being relieved by popping the ears in much the same way as on a plane.

As the distance from the surface increases, so the natural light filtering down fades and soon it is dark and gloomy. The rope the divers are

General arrangement of the MV *Akka*

following down seems to disappear straight down below into the darkness with no end in sight. Pushing on further down, the water clarity starts to improve and very soon the sweep of the divers' torches reveals the silhouette of the stern sitting upright on an even keel, richly covered in colourful plumrose anemones and the white, bulbous dead men's fingers sponges. They have arrived at the stern accommodation superstructure which rises one level above the main deck. This deck-house was once a hive of activity in the *Akka*'s seagoing days. The main deck superstructure held the crew's cabins and the shelter deck level below housed the seamen's and first engineer's mess rooms and toilets and, at the stern itself, the steering gear. A walkway curves its way around the complete circumference of the stern with doors and portholes giving fascinating glimpses inside the wreck. Two of the ship's lifeboats used to swing in their davits above this accommodation, one at either side of the deck-house flanking the crew's bar which was accommodated in a small deck-house on top.

The two derricks and their jibs which formerly stood just forward of this deck-house have been brought crashing down on to the deck by the clearance work on her. Broken off stumps, now covered with sealife, reveal where they once stood. Standing on the deck at her very stern at a depth of 24 metres, the seabed is still some 16 metres below, well out of sight in the inky blackness. Peering over the stern itself, the propeller is missing, having been salvaged in recent years. A few ropes and cables are draped over the side of the hull here, providing a foothold and shelter for anemones.

The *Akka* had six cavernous holds, two aft of the bridge superstructure and four forward. The aftmost holds still have their hatch covers on them although the bow holds are open. They are seemingly bottomless black voids that entice drivers inside. Dropping down into the holds, however, dramatically eats into the available time that the diver can spend on the wreck. The cargo she was carrying when she sunk was iron ore and so an excursion down into the holds is not particularly rewarding.

The gunwhales rise up about three metres from the main deck of the *Akka* and so whilst you are swimming along the deck you feel protected and sheltered from any current that might be running on the wreck. Soon the midships superstructure rears into view. This superstructure originally comprised the main deck-house, the promenade deck, boat deck and, at the very top, the nagivating bridge deck. The 1956 clearance operations removed the top levels of this four-level superstructure.

Beneath this superstructure at shelter deck level can be found the galley, hospital, crew's mess, cook's quarters, pantry and engineer's accommodation. Many items of crockery bearing the *Akka*'s shipping line logo have been recovered from this area. The engine-rooms are located beneath this deck level.

On the main deck, walkways run along either side of the deck-house with gaping doorways opening into cabins and portholes allowing in

Crockery recovere
from the *Akka*'s
galley still bears t
shipping line's log

shafts of light. At the very front of this deck-house can be found the remnants of the lounge to port and the saloon and first officer's cabin to starboard. The row of cabins to either side of this deck-house and the lounge and saloon to the front enclose the motor casing through which the now removed funnel once rose. The midships accommodation here is perhaps the most accessible on the wreck. Much of the plating and most of the decking has rotted away to leave a skeletal framework of struts and spars, creating the illusion of a number of adjoining open boxes through which it is possible to drift and pass from one deck to another. Care must be taken here, however, as the structure seems to be collapsing in places. The clearance operations on her have made it relatively easy to get access to the lower decks and engine-room but great care must be taken. This is serious wreck penetration and should only be undertaken by properly equipped and trained divers. The innards of the *Akka* are vast and confusing. It would be easy for the unwary or inexperienced to become disoriented. The visibility can quickly be destroyed by clouds of silt billowing up from careless fin strokes.

Two further derricks used to stand on the main deck just forward of the midships superstructure. These derricks were also brought crashing down on to the deck by the 1956 clearance works and one of them fell straddling two of the forward holds, Nos 2 and 3, crushing the bulkhead dividing them where it landed. It now acts as a guide, leading divers forward into shallower water as they near the deck-house from where the foremast once rose. It is possible to drop down into the hold forward of the bridge and pass through the gaping, fatal hole ripped out of her port side when she struck the Gantock Rocks in 1956. Scramble nets, flung over the side as the ship went down, are still draped over the port side amidships.

Beyond this and the raised fo'c'sle appears with two doors allowing access into its dark interior. At shelter deck level the carpenter's shop, storerooms, the chain locker and the fore peak tank were housed here. On main deck level were further storerooms. Moving up on top of the fo'c'sle, in amongst the rich covering of dead men's fingers, mooring bollards and deck winches, traces of the white paint that once coated the superstructure can still be made out even after all this time in the depths.

At the bow itself the wreck stops abruptly. Draped over the starboard side of the hull near the bow is an old heavy gauge net which has provided a convenient foothold for dead men's fingers and colonial organisms. There is much damage to the structure of the wreck here on the starboard side. Some time ago another large cardinal navigation buoy was moored so close to the wreck that the large links of the mooring chain used to rub up and down the side of the wreck with the swing of the tide, scouring the hull clean of life and damaging its structure. That buoy is no longer moored here but the damage caused by it in days gone by is clearly visible.

All too soon the permitted time for the diver to stay down, the 'bottom time', is spent and it is time to return slowly to the surface. Reaching upwards, the colourfully adorned steel of the wreck soon merges into the inky blackness below. The divers seem suspended in a void with neither the surface above nor the seabed below visible. The divers keep a watchful eye on their depth gauges. It is only these that can tell the diver whether he is still ascending or whether he has started to sink again. Floating effortlessly in a weightless void, it is easy to lose track of where you are and become disoriented. Only the taut buoy line and the depth gauge reveal that the ascent is continuing. Some excess air is vented from the buoyancy control jacket to slow what could become an accelerating ascent. As a diver rises towards the surface the air in his jacket and his suit expands in volume giving him increased buoyancy and so speeding his rate of ascent. It is essential to ascend slowly to give time for the bubbles of nitrogen, which are expanding at the same rate, to pass freely and safely from the bloodstream. As the diver reaches the upper layers of the Clyde the water, clear below, becomes murky again. Slowly, almost imperceptibly, the natural light filtering down from the surface increases. The divers are almost back at the surface and it is time for a safety decompression stop if required. Soon they are back on the surface and

the dive boat closes in to pick them up and whisk them back to land. It
has been a memorable dive.

Essential Information

Boat launch site: For RIBS the slip at the RNLI boathouse at Largs
waterfront or the slip at Cardwell Bay, Gourock.

Tidal conditions: 0–2 knots.

Visibility: 5–15 metres.

Maximum depth: Seabed at stern 40 metres. Main deck 16–24 metres.

Coastguard: (0475) 29988 or (051) 931 3341.

Police: Inverkip (0475) 521222.

Recompression chambers: Western Infirmary, Glasgow (041) 339 8822
HMS *Neptune*, Faslane, Helensburgh (0436) 4321. Millport Marine
Laboratory (0475) 553 581.

Air supplies: Kip Watersports, Kip Marina, Inverkip (0475) 521281. C &
C Marine Services, Largs Yacht Haven (0475) 687180.

Sea area: Malin.

Hydrographic chart: No 1907, Little Cumbrae to Cloch Point.

Position: Lat 55 56 43.0 N, Long 04 54 20.0 W.

THE *SAN TIBURCIO*
Moray Firth

The *San Tiburcio* was an 8,266 dwt British steam-driven tanker built for
the famous Eagle Fleet in 1921 by Standard Ship Building Corporation at
Shooters Island, New York. She was launched on 29 January 1921 by Mrs
Cornelius W. Wickersham and delivered to the Eagle Oil & Shipping Co.
Ltd on 12 March 1921 and subsequently registered in London. A sizeable
vessel of 5,995 gross tons, 3,618 net, she measured 413 feet in length with
a beam of 53.4 feet and a draught of 31.1 feet. She was constructed of
two steel decks, Web frames and longitudinal framing. Although originally
designed to carry petroleum in bulk, in March 1921 she was fitted out for
carrying oil fuel. Like all tankers past and present the *San Tiburcio* differed
from passenger and cargo ships by having all her engines and associated
machinery fitted at her stern. This arrangement minimised the risk of fire
by keeping the boilers and funnel separated as far as possible from her
highly volatile cargo. If the machinery and boilers were situated amidships
then it would be necessary to run the propeller shaft along an oil-tight
tunnel right through the cargo tanks, creating an obvious risk. Thus the
unusual profile of a tanker with its funnel aft is a direct result of the
nature of its cargo which is both inflammable and also 'searching' or
liable to leak.

The *San Tiburcio* was powered by a triple-expansion steam engine,
the cylinder diameters being 27, 45 and 74 inches and the stroke being 48
inches. She developed a boiler pressure of 180 lb and horsepower of 544
nhp (according to Lloyd's formulae). Her boilers and furnaces were built
by the Sun Shipbuilding Co., Chester, Pennsylvania.

The tankers of the early part of this century were of simple construction.
Basically the tanker was a long steel box divided into a series of
compartments. The forward spaces were designed to carry water, dry
cargo, such as oil in drums, and spare bunkers. The after spaces held
water, bunkers, the cargo pumps and the ship's boilers and engines.
Between these end spaces the rest of the tanker was divided on a gridiron
plan into cargo compartments. The extensive subdivision, sometimes into
as many as 33 separate compartments, gave the tankers exceptional
strength and stability. The war years proved that the tankers could stay

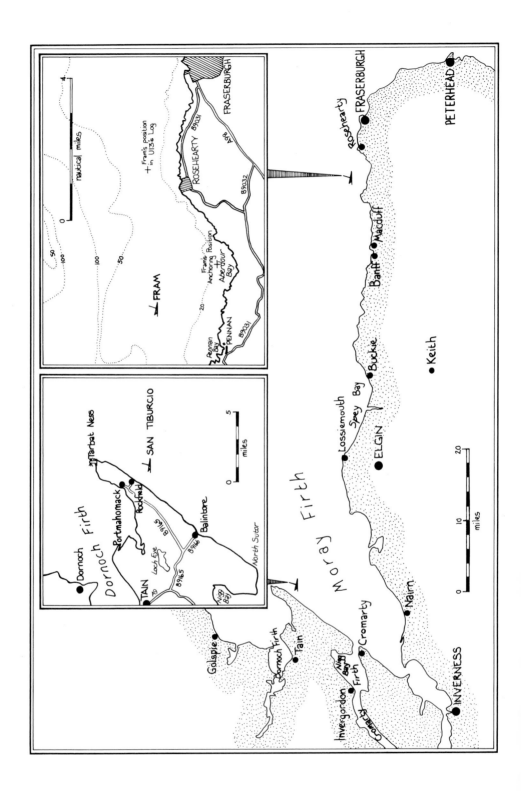

afloat despite more than one large hole being blasted open beneath the waterline.

In hot weather the oil cargo in a tanker expands and in cold weather it contracts. If the ship's tanks were completely sealed this expansion and contraction of the cargo would create a vacuum and dangerous internal pressures. To let the cargo breathe, small pipes came from the top of each tank and ran some way up each of the ship's masts to flameproof outlets high above the deck. At the bottom of the cargo tanks a system of heating coils was installed through which steam was passed if the oil carried was heavy grade which required heating.

Each cargo tank could be filled and emptied independently of the others so that different types of oil could be loaded into separate tanks and discharged without being contaminated. Numerous valves linked every tank to a system of pipelines inside the ship that led to the ship's pumps. Another set of pipelines led up from the pumps on to the tanker's deck where they were conveniently located for connecting to shore pipelines for loading and discharging. The ship's pumps were primarily used for pumping the cargo out of the ship to the shore storage tanks and also for pumping ballast water in or out of the ship. Shore pumps were used for pumping the cargo aboard.

The deck of the *San Tiburcio* was a continuous weather deck only penetrated by small cargo hatches, one for each tank, with watertight

The Eagle Fleet
tanker *San Tiburcio*
(National Maritime
Museum,
Greenwich)

steel lids which were kept sealed down when the ship was loaded. Above this weather deck were three superstructures: the fo'c'sle, the midships deck-house and the poop. The fo'c'sle space was used to store ship's equipment. The midships deck-house held the bridge, chartroom, radio room, storerooms and officers' accommodation. The poop held the rest of the ship's company, mess rooms, galley, refrigerated space and steering gear.

Oil-fired furnaces aboard an Eagle Fleet tanker (courtesy of the Eagle Fleet, Orion Publishing Group Ltd)

These three superstructures were connected by the 'flying bridge', an elevated walkway that ran fore and aft along the centre of the vessel about eight feet above the weather deck. Tankers were permitted to load more deeply because of their subdivision into a large number of watertight compartments. A fully laden tanker would lie deep in the water and in rough weather the weather deck was continually swept by the seas. The tanker would become a three-island ship with only its three superstructures visible, connected to each other by the elevated flying bridge.

At sea the navigation bridge and engine-room had to be manned continuously day and night on a three-watch system, each watch being of four hours' duration. The navigation watch consisted of one navigating officer and three able seamen. The engine-room watch consisted of two engineer officers and two firemen. The rest of the deck and engine ratings worked an eight-hour day under the supervision of their respective petty officers. Saturday afternoons and Sundays were off-duty periods for all ratings except watchkeepers and the catering staff who worked a seven-day week.

The Eagle Fleet was founded in 1912 by Weetman Pearson, first Viscount Cowdray, who staked his personal fortune and reputation to create an oil empire in Mexico. He had gone to Mexico with his wife on

The decks of the *San Alberto* are awash in this moderate south-westerly Atlantic gale but the flying bridge still allows passage from the fo'c'sle to the bridge (courtesy of the Eagle Fleet, Orion Publishing)

holiday in 1889, yet he had hardly arrived there before his active mind was mulling over a potentially lucrative scheme. In true entrepreneurial spirit he conceived a scheme to drain the marshy lands around Mexico City. Within ten days of his arrival he had worked out plans for the colossal task, drawn up estimates and signed contracts with the Mexican Government for the construction of a Grand Canal costing over £2,000,000. Other grandiose projects were to follow as his entrepreneurial spirit spurred him to grasp opportunities as and when he saw them.

It was this same adventuresome spirit that years later would lead him into oil. In April 1901 on his way back from Mexico he had a nine-hour wait at Laredo in Texas to catch a connecting train to New York. Laredo was caught in the frenzy of an oil rush and prospectors were pouring into town. Seeing yet another business opportunity, he filled his nine-hour wait studying all the prospectuses and all the information he could get hold of locally. He had never been involved in oil before but was adept at recognising a good business opportunity and unafraid to gamble on such a scheme. Before he caught his connection he had cabled his manager in Mexico and arranged for him to secure an option on as much land as he could in the neighbourhood of San Cristobal on the Isthmus of Tehuantepec.

From this chance beginning an oil production empire was created. As the years passed this empire expanded rapidly and soon Pearson realised that the long-term security of his Mexican oil interests depended not only on his ability to produce the oil but also the ability to distribute and sell it. It was this far-sighted and perceptive realisation that led him to found the Eagle Oil fleet. Initially he bought two tanker steamers and renamed them *San Cristobal* and *San Bernardo* after two saints in the Mexican

church calendar. (Subsequently all Eagle Fleet ships would be named following this precedent.) By 1912 the demand for his Mexican oil had outstripped this infant fleet. Not being a man to take half measures, he founded Eagle Oil Transport Company, with a capital of £3,000,000. Orders were immediately placed at British yards for the construction of 19 new tankers. The Eagle Oil Fleet was going to be big business.

The outbreak of World War I saw tumultuous times for the Eagle Oil Fleet. Mexican oil production trebled to meet the demand from the Allies but sadly five of the Fleet were sunk by enemy action. At the end of the war, in 1919, a five-year building programme was prepared with a view to doubling the size of the pre-war fleet. Twenty-five new ships were to be launched, 14 of which, including the *San Tiburcio*, were to be 8,000 to 9,000-dwt vessels due to be launched between 1921 and 1924.

With characteristic foresight, Eagle Oil had opened offices in Rio de Janeiro and Buenos Aires in 1913 after their analysts had identified a growing market in South America. Now, in the post-war years, trade with South America boomed as the continent became a major international oil purchaser. The shallow draughts of the smaller tankers such as the *San Tiburcio* made them able to navigate the shallow channels through the River Plate estuary and reach the shallower ports further up river where the larger 15,000-ton tankers could not pass.

In the decade that followed the construction of the *San Tiburcio* there was, however, a calamitous decline in Mexican oil output. This fall in

Main deck of the San Delfino showing the Flying Bridge walkway. The deck is twisted out of alignment after she struck a mine in December 1939 (courtesy of the Eagle Fleet, Orion, Publishing)

output at a time when demand was increasing forced heavy buying of oil from the Californian fields. For many years Eagle Fleet tankers were profitably engaged loading oil at San Pedro in California and shipping it to Mexico for refining. After discharging their cargo here they would then be loaded with refined products and sail for Rio, Santos, Montevideo and Buenos Aires to supply the eager South American market. Once unloaded, they would then return in ballast through the Straits of Magellan to San Pedro, in all a round trip of 100 days. The Eagle Fleet suffered many a bad year in these tumultuous times, the worst being 1925, 1931 and 1932 when between five and ten per cent of their ships were idle.

The *San Tiburcio* was destined to sail the seas for 19 years before meeting her end far from her normal trade routes in the Moray Firth in the north-east of Scotland on 4 May 1940 in Britain's first year of the war. She was one of many of the losses that the Eagle Fleet suffered as the Axis forces tried to strangle Britain's war machine by cutting off precious oil supplies. In total 16 tankers, totalling 250,000 tons of shipping and nearly two-thirds of the Eagle Fleet, were destroyed by enemy action and another seven seriously damaged.

The *San Tiburcio* had, by this time, been chartered by the Ministry of War Transport and set off on what was to be her final voyage from Scapa Flow, the deep, sheltered Royal Navy anchorage in the Orkney Islands of Scotland, under the command of Captain W.F. Fynn. She was loaded with a cargo of 2,193 tons of fuel oil and 12 aeroplane floats, bound for the port of Invergordon in the Cromarty Firth, the sheltered inlet that runs off the Moray Firth itself. The crew envisaged a relatively short journey of a day or two down the north-east coast of Scotland as they readied the *San Tiburcio* for sea. Gently she left her mooring and moved southwards across the wide expanse of deep water that is Scapa Flow. She had soon passed southwards through the steel anti-submarine boom nets that were stretched across Hoxa Sound and Switha Sound, the main entrances and exits to the Flow. A well-worn procedure had moved smoothly into operation. On a prearranged set of visual signals with the Port War Signal Station at Stanger Head in Flotta, a section of the boom net was swung open by a boom patrol vessel to let the *San Tiburcio* pass out of the heavily guarded naval anchorage and into the Pentland Firth.

On leaving the Flow by this southerly exit the *San Tiburcio* headed east along the Pentland Firth, the notorious stretch of dangerous sea that divides the Orkney Islands from mainland Scotland. The Pentland Firth was not swept for mines by the Royal Navy as the Admiralty felt that, with the shore defences and the considerable volume of Allied traffic using this narrow stretch of water, no German surface vessel or minelaying submarine would dare enter to lay mines. The swept channel which ran down the east coast of Scotland began at Duncansby Head, the very north-east tip of Scotland. It was approximately half to one mile wide and lay eight miles offshore, marked by buoys every ten miles.

At this time the Northern Mine Barrage was being extended from just north of Fraserburgh up to the Orkneys. The existing mine barrage extended in a line from the Thames Estuary northwards to Fraserburgh and was deployed further out into the North Sea than the swept channel. This defensive mine barrier was designed to protect coastal shipping against incursions by enemy surface vessels or submarines. German minelaying vessels had already demonstrated their capacities and shown great daring in laying their mines which had taken a heavy toll on coastal Allied shipping. However, the extension of the mine barrier northwards, from Fraserburgh to Orkney, would not come soon enough for *San Tiburcio*.

As Duncansby Head passed by to starboard and the *San Tiburcio* altered her course to run down the swept channel along the north-east coast, she soon passed Wick on her starboard beam and continued southwards until the southmost promontory of the Dornoch Firth, Tarbat Ness, came into view. Passing on beyond Tarbat Ness, she entered the sheltered waters of the Moray Firth. The crew could see right across the wide expanse of the Firth to Burghead in the distance to the south. Journey's end was almost in sight for them as Invergordon lay only a few miles away. In a few hours' time the crew would be berthing the *San Tiburcio* and offloading her valuable cargo. But these thoughts were premature: 4 May 1940 would be the *San Tiburcio*'s last day afloat.

Soon Tarbat Ness was about four miles off in the distance on her starboard side and the small fishing village of Rockfield could be made out ashore. Suddenly there was a tremendous explosion amidships and a column of water rose upwards. The *San Tiburcio* had struck a mine.

Some three months earlier, on 9 February 1940, the 329-ton Type IIB German minelaying submarine *U 9*, under the command of FK (Fregatten Kapitän) Wolfgang Lüth, had slipped unseen through these waters. Lüth had deployed her complement of eight contact mines and then guided *U 9* away from the area undetected. *U 9*'s mines were laid at a depth of about eight metres; enough to allow small coastal vessels to pass over them safely. There was little point in wasting a valuable mine on a small fishing boat when it was intended for much bigger prey. For three months

Type IIB German submarine *U 9* (bear ing a commemorative Iron Cross) tha laid the fateful min which sunk the *San Tiburcio*. Over 140 feet long with a beam of 13 feet and a draught of 14 feet, she displaced 279 tons on the surface and 329 submerged Driven by two diese motors on the surface she developed 700 bhp and could make 13 knots, giv ing her an operatin radius of 1,800 mile Submerged, she ran on electric motors developing 360 bhp and pushing her along at seven kno (although her operat ing radius was reduced to 43 mile at four knots). She was fitted with one 20-mm AA gun an three 21-inch bow torpedo tubes. Whe used operationally her armament was increased to four 2 mm AA guns (2 × 2 She carried six torp does or eight mine and had a crew of 2

the mines had lain in wait for an unsuspecting victim.

Immediately after the explosion the *San Tiburcio* started flooding with water and settling into the sea. As the water rushed into her innards her natural buoyancy was disrupted and her structure, strong and secure when properly supported by the sea in normal conditions, became subjected to stresses and strains that it could not cope with. With the increasing amount of water flooding into her, the strain became intolerable and she broke her back at the tanker's weakest point; just aft of midships. The hull broke almost in a clean line straight across the deck from one side of the hull to the other as though cut with a knife. Her two halves did not sink immediately as other vessels might have done. Her system of watertight compartments managed to keep the two sections afloat for 45 minutes before the devastated *San Tiburcio* passed from sight. Thankfully, none of the crew was injured in the explosion and after staying afloat for so long they were able to get off her in safety. There was no loss of life.

The bow and stern sections of the *San Tiburcio* plunged down through the cold waters to the seabed more than 30 metres below, both settling on even keels. The bow section, some 160 feet long, settled in a roughly north/south direction with the bow pointing south. The stern section of some 255 feet settled almost at right angles to the bow section about 30 metres away.

U 9 was later transferred to the Black Sea, probably in sections via the River Danube, and was eventually bombed and sunk by Allied warplanes at Constanza on 20 August 1944.

Within days of the *San Tiburcio* sinking, on about 18 May 1940, a green Dan buoy was laid about 500 yards north-east of the wreck, although because of the depth of the wreck it was not considered to be a hazard to navigation. The buoy remained in place for 18 years until May 1958 when it was decided to remove it, as presumably by then all hope had been given up of salvaging the wreck. The *San Tiburcio* was to all intents and purposes then forgotten about and lay undisturbed in her watery tomb for nearly 20 years until local divers started diving her in the early 1970s. In 1976 a two-boat drift sweep was made over her. The sweep was clear at 19.1 metres but fouled at 19.8 metres.

The boom in sport diving of the 1970s and 1980s resulted in the *San Tiburcio* becoming a very popular dive for the local clubs. The reports from divers over the years have shown that the two sections of the *San Tiburcio* are now decaying fairly rapidly and she is beginning to break up in places. In 1984 it was reported that her tanks were still full of oil although this conflicts with reports from local divers who are certain that the tanks were empty as far back as 1973. In 1989 Royal Navy divers used high explosives to blast the large stern gun from its mount on the stern accommodation. The blast caused quite an amount of damage and caused a large amount of oil to leak from the stern section. The cargo tanks at this time were reported to be empty and it was assumed that the oil was leaking from engine fuel tanks immediately beneath which had been damaged by the blast. Scattered around in the debris at the location of the gun mount at the stern were left at least 20 high-explosive shells. These were inspected by Ordnance Disposal experts who considered them to be very dangerous if removed from the water. It is understood that they have now all safely been recovered and disposed of. The hatches on the bow section have also been blown off and the cargo tanks here too are now empty.

Today the wreck of the *San Tiburcio* can be found at Latitude 57 46 34.0 N and Longitude 003 45 32.0 W about four miles south from the distinctive Tarbat Ness lighthouse which bears 003 degrees from the wreck site. Rockfield, the small coastal village about two to three miles south-west along the coast from Tarbat Ness, is the closest land settlement to the site. Both sections of the wreck are usually marked with a small buoy and give good magnetometer and echo-sounder readings.

The *San Tiburcio* is now regularly dived upon and hard-boat dive charters can be taken from Nairn, Cromarty and Balintore. The closest launch site for a dive boat, be it RIB or hard boat, is the typically picturesque fishing village of Balintore on the north side of the Firth. From here it is a hard-boat journey of 40 minutes, depending on the seas, and 20 minutes for an RIB. There is a good harbour and slip although the harbour is very tidal, drying out at low water. The small town of Cromarty on the Black Isle has a good, small, sheltered harbour which can be used at most states of the tide and there is also a slip beside the lighthouse. From Cromarty it is a scenic trip by boat past stacked oil supply platforms out through the narrow neck of the Cromarty Firth. On the hills at either side of the entrance to the Firth deserted gun emplacements, relics of World War II, still cover shipping with wide fields of fire from their elevated sites. The hard-boat trip to the site from Cromarty will take well in excess of an hour. A similar trip of more than one hour will take a hard boat from Nairn across to the site. Nairn does have a slip for RIBs to be launched from but it, like Balintore, is a very tidal harbour for hard boats which results in the departure and return time having to be timed to coincide with there being enough water in the harbour. There is also a small slip in Findhorn Bay suitable for launching and retrieving RIBs.

Most of the local skippers know the location of the wreck of the *San Tiburcio* and often take sea angling parties out to her. The wreck of the *San Tiburcio* has become an artificial reef, supporting a varied marine ecosystem and providing safe refuge and food for countless fish. The skippers are equally happy to take divers out to the site which, although buoyed, can be difficult to find when the seas are running.

THE BOW SECTION

The 160-foot bow section lies on an even keel in about 30–35 metres of water in an approximate north/south direction with the bow pointing

The wreck of the
tanker *San Tiburcio*

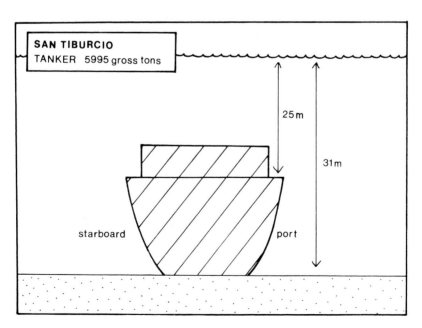

SAN TIBURCIO
TANKER   5995 gross tons

25 m

31 m

starboard   port

south. Just aft of the midships superstructure and bridge this section of the wreck stops abruptly where she broke in two. About 30 metres away from the tangled and jagged edges of this area lies the larger stern section. Both sections of the wreck are now decaying quite heavily. The hull itself is intact but the thinner steel of the superstructure has all but rusted away, leaving an open framework of ribs and spars.

At the very tip of the bow the sturdy flag pole on top of the fo'c'sle still remains in place, now heavily covered with sealife and often providing a convenient mooring point for a marker buoy. This fo'c'sle space was used during the ship's seagoing days to store equipment although the easily accessible spaces are now all empty. At either side of the fo'c'sle the hull is lined with portholes and the port side anchor hangs from its hawse. The seabed around the bow of the wreck shows much impact damage resulting from the bow section, filled with oil fuel, ploughing into the bed as it plunged down from the surface. Although the average seabed depth is 30–35 metres the impact damage and tidal scouring have created a depression at the bow where divers have reported depths of 41 metres. On top of the forecastle there is a heavy winch and a raised hatch and cover which allowed access down into it. Moving aft, the fo'c'sle ends with a drop down to the main weather deck. The foremast was originally situated here but it would appear to have been blasted and removed, presumably to minimise the danger to shipping. Only a small section of about ten feet of the foremast remains before it ends abruptly in a mangle of blasted steel.

To the starboard side of the deck there is a small deck-house with two open doorways into it. The rooms inside are now empty and thickly covered with silt. All over the deck the intricate system of multi-sized interconnecting pipes linking all the cargo spaces to the ship's pumps can be seen. Larger pipes run fore and aft along either side of the deck and along the centre line of the deck. These pipes lead to the small pumphouse superstructure located on the centre line of the vessel, just in front of the bridge superstructure. From here further pipes exit aft and run at deck level through the bridge superstructure towards the tanks aft of the bridge. Most of the oil tank hatches on the bow section have been blown off in the past and the cargo tanks, like the stern tanks, are now empty. A few of the hatches still have their covers on them, still firmly clamped down.

The main profusion of larger pipes runs fore and aft along the centre line of the weather deck. About eight feet above the deck a second layer of pipes run fore and aft. On top of these, parts of the 'flying bridge' walkway that linked the top of the fo'c'sle to the bridge superstructure can still be made out. This walkway was flanked at either side by handrails and although these have in the main rusted away, some of the spars still remain to give an idea of the set-up of this feature. Originally the 'flying bridge' reached the bridge superstructure at promenade deck level where further steps at the front of the superstructure led up to the boat deck and open bridge.

The main section of the bridge superstructure originally rose three levels above the weather deck with, at either side of the roof of the bridge, two small open observation posts and a larger central communications room centered on top. With the ravages of 50 years' immersion in the Moray Firth the thinner steel that enclosed these superstructure spaces has rotted away, leaving a virtually open framework of rooms that the diver can pass through with ease. Above, the roofing has gone, leaving only the structural spars and struts and allowing easy entry and exit points from the rooms below. The open bridge was located on the boat deck, level three of this superstructure. Behind this open bridge a row of portholes from the dry bridge looked out forward. A row of portholes also lined the bulkhead on the deck level beneath. This deck-house held the bridge, chartroom, radio room, storerooms and officers' accommodation. Many interesting pieces of crockery and old bottles have been recovered from this area. Two of the ship's lifeboats originally swung in davits just behind the bridge, one at either side of the hull.

Moving further aft, the same pattern of oil pipes running fore and aft along the deck is visible. The deck, however, does not go very far before it ends abruptly perhaps 20 or 30 feet aft of the bridge. Here is the cataclysmic tear in the weather deck where the *San Tiburcio* broke her back after striking the mine. It is almost as though her deck has been cut across from one side of her hull to the other with a knife, so true and straight is the cut. The edges of the break are frayed and bent downwards like cardboard as a result of the awesome forces that tore this vessel in two.

This marks the end of the bow section. When the visibility is good the blurred outline of the start of the stern section at right angles to the bow can be made out 30 metres away.

THE STERN SECTION

The stern section of the *San Tiburcio* at about 250 feet long is somewhat larger than the bow section. It rests on an even keel in about 30–35 metres of water. Quite often there is a buoy or empty oil drum tied off on a convenient roof strut on the stern superstructure itself. The actual stern is covered with a profusion of sponges, soft corals and anemones, a breathtaking sight as it curves round and plunges down towards the seabed. The visibility here is an average 10 metres and so from the roof of this deck-house and often from the weather deck the seabed is usually still out of sight in the darkness below.

The two most significant features of this section from the ship's days afloat have now gone. The large distinctive funnel was originally situated at the front bulkhead of the stern deck-house but has long since corroded and rotted away. In its heyday the funnel was a distinctive feature of the Eagle Fleet with its striking black and gold bands and below a broad white band with the fleet's trademark, a large golden eagle, emblazoned on it. The mainmast has been removed in the past, presumably with the foremast to minimise the danger to shipping above. There is little trace of the covered walkway that once ringed its way around the complete deck-house.

During the *San Tiburcio*'s short war service the Admiralty mounted a large gun on the roof of the stern deck-house. It would probably have been a four-inch gun and was intended to fire astern on an enemy, such as a U-boat, pursuing her as she tried to use her speed to outrun her foe. The stern gun was removed by a Royal Navy team using explosives in 1989.

Moving forward over the aft accommodation, near the forward bulkhead the metal decking and bulkheads have rotted away, allowing safe and easy access through the various interconnecting rooms and passageways in the upper level. Divers can pass safely through large openings in the roofs and walls of these rooms and become familiar with the internal layout of the deck-house. This deck-house rose up for two deck levels above the weather deck and originally housed the crew's accommodation, mess rooms, galley, refrigerated space and, below decks, the engine-room and steering gear. Here and there in these rooms can be found ominous-looking manholes leading down into the bowels of the vessel to the engine and boiler rooms below. Thankfully these are too tight to allow a bulky diver with his cumbersome suit and air cylinder on his back to get into. There is therefore no real incentive to entice divers to do deep wreck penetration, which is only for properly equipped and trained experts. Scattered about the floor are small, silt-covered piles of small brass engine-room and pipe fitments, obviously the result of some small-scale salvage work in the past.

Passing out through one of the doors in the forward bulkhead of the top level of this deck-house there is a staggered drop to the deck level below. Ladders and steps which would have allowed the crew to quickly rise up and down the two deck levels are still welded to the bulkhead. On the weather deck below the general depth is about 26 metres at low water and 30 metres at high. Here can be located the tanker's spare propellers, still chained securely to the deck.

Moving forward on the weather deck the same regular pattern of larger pipes running fore and aft (as on the bow section) resumes. Here and there large circular valves interrupt the regular lines. A small deck-house straddles the pipes just forward of the stern superstructure. The 'flying bridge' gangway that ran about eight feet above the deck, linking the bridge deck-house and the stern deck-house, is still complete and now covered in sponges. In bad visibility it is a good guide forward and back to the shot line at the stern. Some of the small hatches for the cargo tanks, some six feet across, have been blown off in the past with explosives. Others are still in place but the tanks themselves are now empty. At either side of the deck there is a raised bulwark rail. The hull itself is covered in dead men's fingers and sponges for as far as the eye can see. So thick is the covering that the whole side of the hull appears as a huge white wall. There is hardly a gap where the original steel of the hull itself can be seen. The brilliant blaze of white drops straight down towards the seabed some five–ten metres below and out of sight, except on days when the visibility is particularly good.

The flat expanse of the deck seems to run off into infinity but stops suddenly in a jagged line where the vessel split in two as she sank. It is possible here to drop down below the weather deck to investigate the innards and rugged construction of this once proud lady of the seas.

Essential Information

Boat launch site: RIBs and hard-boat charters at Nairn, Cromarty, Findhorn and Balintore. Tidal harbours with little water at low water.
Tidal conditions: 0–0.7 knots.
Visibility: 10–30 metres. 15 metres average.
Maximum depth: Weather deck 30 metres at high water, 25 at low. Seabed 31 metres at low, 35 at high. Bow 41 metres.
Coastguard: Aberdeen (0224) 592334.
Police: Nearest continuously manned stations are at Tain (0862) 892215, Alness (0349) 882222.
Air supplies: Hard-boat charters have onboard compressors. Nearest local compressor is owned by Inverness BSAC. Contact George Brown, Expeditions Officer on (0463) 240529 to make arrangements.
Sea area: Cromarty. Telephone Coastguard or Met Office for Inshore Forecast.
Recompression chamber: National Hyperbaric Centre, Aberdeen (0224) 698895.
Hydrographic chart: No 223, Dunrobin Point to Buckie.
Position: Lat 57 46 34 N, Long 03 45 32 W.

THE *FRAM*
Aberdour Bay, Moray Firth

The Swedish steel steamship *Fram* was built by Sir Raylton Dixon & Co., in Middlesbrough in 1897 for the Danish-Russian Steamship Co. at a cost of 532,507 Danish Kroner. Originally known as the *Russ*, she boasted a gross tonnage of 2,491, an underdeck tonnage of 2,297 and a net tonnage of 1,525. The *Russ* was a sizeable one-decked vessel, 314.7 feet in length with a beam of 43 feet and a draught of 20.5 feet. She was powered by triple-expansion engines (with cylinder diameters of 22, 36 and 60 inches and a stroke of 42 inches) built by G. Clark Ltd of Sunderland which developed a powerful 233 nhp. She carried a crew of 19.

The *Russ* led a long and useful life at sea in a variety of different incarnations before her seagoing days came to a sudden and tragic end in the cold waters of the Moray Firth near Rosehearty in 1940. In her early years as part of the Danish-Russian Steamship Co.'s fleet she carried cargoes of wood and pulp around the ports of the Baltic Sea. On 16 April 1920 the Danish-Russian Steamship Co. and its complete fleet was taken over by Det Forenede Dampskibsselskab of Kobenhoun. Following hard on the heels of that deal the *Russ* was then sold on to Angfartyg A/B 'Kjell' based in Kalmar in Sweden and was then renamed the *Fram*. Although she was already by then an old vessel with 23 years' service at sea, she remained under the Swedish flag, profitably carrying cargoes for yet another 20 years. In those years she was involved in two sea collisions, firstly with the Norwegian steamship *Hessa* and latterly with the English steamer *Continental Trader*. In 1937 the *Fram*'s port of registration was changed to Stockholm. By the time that World War II unleashed its carnage over Europe the *Fram* was a venerable old lady of the seas with more than 40 years' service at sea.

In those 40 years since her construction, technology had progressed far, leaving the *Fram* as a slow, cumbersome vessel in comparison to the modern ships of the times. She had a cruising speed of only nine to ten knots but still was able to fulfil a useful wartime role pushing cargoes from one port to another. Her long sea career, however, would come to a sudden and tragic end on 1 February 1940 when she would be blown in two in a catastrophic explosion and sent to the bottom. A single torpedo strike amidships by a small coastal U-boat, *U 13*, fatally wounded her and consigned her to the lengthening statistics of wartime shipping losses.

The tangled web of history and chance that led to the *Fram*'s demise on that cold February morning is lengthy and complicated. The trail can even be traced back to the momentous events at Scapa Flow at the end of World War I. On the 21 June 1919 the 74 warships that made up the German Imperial Navy's High Seas Fleet scuttled themselves at Scapa Flow in the Orkney Islands off northern Scotland in the mistaken belief that the fighting, temporarily suspended on 11 November 1918 by the Armistice, was about to recommence. The entire fleet, interned there by the Allies for seven long months, dramatically sank to the bottom of the Flow in one of the most famous acts of naval suicide ever. Ironically, on the 28 June 1919, just seven days later, the Treaty of Versailles was signed by the Allies and Germany, formally ending World War I.

Germany's military strength was severely curtailed by the Treaty but in the years leading up to World War II the Anglo-German Naval Agreement had been signed and Germany had been allowed to start building a navy again. Germany had, however, been secretly developing the U-boat in Holland since 1922, even though that was a clear breach of the Treaty of Versailles. It was only as late as March 1935 that Hitler publicly repudiated the Treaty of Versailles and U-boat production went into full swing. Within one year of that repudiation the German naval yard at Kiel had produced 14 U-boats.

In 1939 it was announced that Karl Dönitz, who had been the one and only U-boat flotilla commander since 1935, was to command the new submarine arm of the Germany Navy, the Kriegsmarine. German Command believed, however, that it would be years, perhaps as many as ten, before the Kriegsmarine, and, in particular, the newly formed U-boat Arm, would be powerful enough to take on the might of the British Royal Navy.

When war was declared Dönitz had under his command only 56 U-boats of which only 20 or so were suitable for the Atlantic. Six months later, by the beginning of 1940, his fleet had been reduced to a dangerously low level of 32 U-boats by the effective British sub-hunters. Those U-boats that did break out into the Atlantic had to return to Germany round the north coast of Scotland and run the gauntlet in the shallow reaches of the North Sea. (With the occupation of France later in 1940 they could then base themselves on the long west coast of France which gave unlimited access to the deep, open waters of the Atlantic, more safely and much more quickly.)

As January 1940 gave way to February a south-easterly gale had been blowing over the Moray Firth, bringing high winds and snow storms. The gale had lasted for several days already and in the exposed, open waters of the North Sea conditions were horrific. Many vessels had run for the shelter of the southerly coast of the Moray Firth to find a respite from the intolerable sea conditions. The Moray Firth is generally bypassed by the heavy sea traffic running up and down the east coast of Scotland but fate had decreed that two vessels would meet in the Firth that night. Only one would be afloat the following day. Within a matter of a few weeks of the *Fram*'s sinking Dönitz would order all his U-boats away from their Atlantic patrols for a period of three months to assist with the invasion of Norway. For the unfortunate *Fram*, however, that period of respite from the scavenging U-boats would not come quickly enough.

The *Fram* had set out on a voyage from Stockholm to Hartlepool, Cleveland, just to the south of Newcastle, in ballast, her holds filled with boulders. She had struggled against heavy seas as she made her way up the west coast of Sweden, passing through the *Kattegat*, the strip of water that separates Denmark from Sweden. Once through the *Kattegat* she had passed out into the open waters of the *Skagerrak* and then onwards, battling against the mountainous waters of the North Sea. The crossing had taken three days and the south-easterly gale had made conditions difficult and arduous. With little sign of the storm abating, the captain had decided to take refuge from the gales and ride out the storm in the relatively sheltered waters of the Moray Firth.

Once the extreme north-east tip of Scotland, Fraserburgh in Aberdeenshire, was sighted, the *Fram* moved along the coastline for about seven miles until she was out of the worst of the weather. She anchored in the lee of the land, about two-and-a-half miles offshore in Aberdour Bay, just to the west of the small fishing village of Rosehearty. In this sheltered anchorage she found some respite from the fierce winds and heavy seas. The foul weather would, in time, blow itself out and allow the *Fram* to continue her scheduled voyage down the east coast of Scotland to Hartlepool. Her approximate anchoring position according to coastguard reports of the time was Latitude 57 41 00 N, Longitude 02 11 00 W and she is reported to have been lying some 2.3 miles out to sea on a bearing of 259 degrees from a nearby land reference point, Pitsligo Flagstaff. (The log of the U-boat, *U 13*, which sank her puts her in a different location at position 57.43 N and 02.06 W.)

As 31 January passed at midnight to 1 February, one solitary crewman was wearily doing the anchor watch whilst the rest of the crew, fatigued from days of this foul weather, had already turned in. The crew would soon be violently jolted from their sleep by every seaman's worst nightmare: a torpedo attack.

U 13 was a small coastal submarine built in 1935 as Germany frantically armed herself for the conflict she would initiate only four years later. She was a Type II B U-boat, the same class as *U 9* which sank the *San Tiburcio*. She displaced 279 tons on the surface and 329 submerged. Driven by two shaft 700 bhp diesel motors on the surface she could achieve surface speeds of 13 knots. Whilst submerged she ran her electric motors which developed 360 bhp and which could push her along at seven knots. Running on the surface, she had a radius of 1,800 miles at 12 knots. Submerged, her radius was cut to 43 miles at four knots. She was armed with one 20-mm gun and three 21-inch bow torpedo tubes. She carried six torpedoes or, alternatively, eight mines.

Although the war was still young, *U 13* had already seen a fair amount of action before she slipped into the Moray Firth from the North Sea, possibly to find some shelter herself from the atrocious weather conditions. Under her previous commanding officer, Kapitan Leutnant Daublebsky von Eichain, she had lain a minefield off the East Anglian coast on 4 September 1939 which resulted in the loss of three ships later in the month. The rugged north-east of Scotland too was an old hunting ground for *U 13*. Some three months earlier, on 30 October 1939, *U 13*, still under the charge of Kapitan Leutnant von Eichain, had sunk the first of some 50 vessels lost through enemy action in the waters around the north-east coast of Scotland during World War II. *U 13* had come across a small southbound convoy running down the north-east coast about three miles offshore near Rattray Head in Aberdeenshire. The last vessel in the convoy was the 4,666-ton Newcastle steamer *Cairnmona* nearing the end of a long voyage from Canada with a cargo of wheat and copper. *U 13* manoeuvred for position and then launched a torpedo which struck the *Cairnmona* with devastating effect. Just after 11 p.m. lookouts at the nearby coastguard station saw the *Cairnmona* rocked by a large explosion at an approximate position of 57.83 00 N and 01.45 00 W. She immediately started settling quickly down into the water. The coastguard alerted the Peterhead lifeboat station and within 15 minutes the Peterhead lifeboat had been launched and was speeding along the coast in a frantic race against time to save lives. Most of the crew were, however, picked up by the Aberdeen trawler *River Lossie* (A 332) under the charge of skipper James K. Robertson and were transferred to the Peterhead lifeboat when it arrived at the scene of the sinking. In all 42 survivors were picked up and taken safely ashore. Three of the engine-room crew were lost, possibly in the initial explosion.

Three months later, *U 13* was scavenging for prey once again around the north-east coast of Scotland under the command of a new officer, Kapitan Leutnant Schulte. As in the past this would be a rich area of operation for *U 13*. On 31 January 1940, the very day before she sank the *Fram*, *U 13* was in action with devastating effect in the North Sea between Middlesbrough and Bergen. She fell upon the 1,168-ton Norwegian steamer *Start* built in 1923. With deadly accuracy her torpedoes struck a fatal blow to the *Start* and sent her and her crew to the bottom. *U 13* then set off on a bearing that would take her to the sheltered waters of the Moray Firth where she would inflict further human suffering and tragedy to the crew of the *Fram* in Aberdour Bay.

As *U 13* approached Aberdour Bay in the dead of night she would probably have been running on the surface, using the cover of darkness to allow her to charge the batteries for her two 360-bhp electric motors and, at the same time, flush fresh air through her stale, foul-smelling hull. Running on the surface she could travel much faster and cover greater distances.

Just after midnight in the early hours of 1 February a vigilant lookout, scanning the waters and skies around the *U 13*, spotted a large vessel in the distance. The *Fram* had been sighted, lying stationary at anchor in Aberdour Bay as the seas dashed against her old riveted hull plates. Kapitan Leutnant Schulte immediately called the crew of *U 13* to action stations and started manoeuvring his U-boat to get into the best possible firing position at the *Fram*, a beam shot. As *U 13* closed on its prey there was no sign from aboard the *Fram* that the hunter had been sighted. The unsuspecting *Fram* was all too easy a target for *U 13*. By 0043 hours GMT, *U 13* was in position and Schulte gave the order to fire. A single torpedo was launched at the distant prey and ran straight and true towards the unknowing *Fram*. German eyes on the bridge of *U 13* strained in the darkness, watching the torpedo trail streaking towards the *Fram*, eagerly anticipating the outcome of their actions.

The torpedo hit the hull of the *Fram* dead amidships, perhaps penetrating her old hull plates before detonating. The explosion lit up the night sky and a tell-tale plume of water rose upwards in a white, shimmering cascade. Aboard, the explosion wreaked havoc in the bridge, chartroom and central accommodation area and the funnel was destroyed. The ship's lifeboats were also destroyed and two of the dinghies were lost. The air was filled with the sound of metal being torn and rent apart as the structure of the *Fram* was destroyed. Almost immediately she had split into two sections, both starting to fill with seawater and sink.

After witnessing the results of its attack, *U 13* submerged in the deep water of 40 to 50 metres and quickly left the scene. The attack may have been witnessed ashore or, alternatively, the radio operator might have managed to get off a distress signal. Soon there could be allied vessels or planes swarming over the scene of the attack. *U 13* left the area as quickly as possible to search out further prey for her remaining torpedoes.

Aboard the *Fram*, the unfortunate crew, who had nearly all been sleeping below decks, suddenly found themselves pitched from their bunks by the explosion. All power and lighting systems were immediately destroyed and below decks the ship was pitched into complete darkness. In the inky blackness the crew scrambled to find their way up on deck before she went down. Jolted from the warmth of sleep they instantly found themselves far out at sea, struggling for their lives in the freezing winter night as the *Fram*, once solid and secure, split into two sections before their eyes and started to settle quickly into the water.

The crew were quite literally split up with the *Fram*, some on the bow section and the remainder on the stern section. The bow section of the *Fram*, held fast in position by her anchor, was rapidly filling with water and settling down into the water. The stern section, however, unimpeded by any anchor chains, started to drift freely before the high wind and seas. It was settling less quickly into the sea than the bow section and would remain afloat for almost 30 minutes, drifting before the prevailing south-easterly winds for another one-and-a-half miles out to sea before sinking.

The lifeboats had been shattered in the chaos of the torpedo explosion and so the crew were forced to take their chances in the freezing cold seas and launched rafts from both sections. Had anyone ashore seen or heard the attack and raised the alarm? It was unlikely in the small hours of the morning. The sound of the explosion would have been carried away from the land by the south-easterly winds. Those same winds would also work against the rafts and carry them away from the land. The crew's panic-stricken minds raced with a thousand questions as they took to the two rafts and abandoned ship.

The same winds and currents that had taken the drifting stern section of the *Fram* further out to sea also conspired to carry the raft from the bow section well out to sea, away from any land. In the darkness there was little hope of their tiny raft being spotted even if the original attack had been seen and the alarm raised. In all, the men on the bow raft would spend 12 long hours exposed to the elements, grimly clinging to life on their small raft.

The coming of the cold winter's dawn the next day found the survivors drifting well out into the Moray Firth. They could see the Aberdeenshire coast far in the distance but as the morning progressed their spirits sagged as no rescue vessels appeared to pluck them from the freezing raft to safety. At about one p.m. the crew of the 110-foot Aberdeen trawler *Viking Deeps* (A 542), quite unaware of the plight of the crew of the *Fram*, were hard at work on just another monotonous trip. The 226-ton *Viking Deeps* was an old trawler completed in April 1916 at the height of World War I by J. Duthie Torry Shipbuilding Co. Known originally as the *Vale of Forth*, she had been taken up for minesweeping by the Royal Navy and served until 1919 when she was released. She had then been sold to the Bon Accord Steam Fishing Co. Ltd and renamed *Loch Brora*. In 1939 she had been bought by George Robb & Sons Ltd and renamed *Viking Deeps*, one of a class of many *Viking* trawlers. Having served faithfully in World War I, she now found herself, 21 years later, playing a role in another global confrontation.

Suddenly an alert crewman on the *Viking Deeps* spotted the small raft drifting helplessly about ten miles offshore, north of Troup Head. The prevailing south-easterly winds had blown the raft almost eight miles further out into the Moray Firth from the *Fram*'s original anchoring position. As each hour passed, their raft had been drifting further away from land as exhaustion and hypothermia had set in. By the time they were picked up the elements had taken their toll and only five men remained alive. The *Viking Deeps* immediately headed for the nearby port of Macduff where the men were landed and taken to hospital. The survivors, thankful to be alive, were able to relate the story of the night-time U-boat attack to the authorities and also advise them of the remaining crewmen and stewardess aboard the other raft.

There was, however, no trace as yet of the stern raft. At 8.35 a.m. the following day, 2 February, on the second day after the sinking, the

The wreck of the
stern section of the
steamship *Fram*

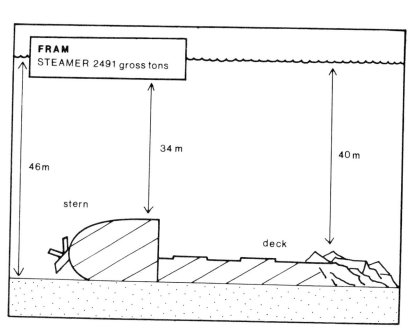

FRAM
STEAMER 2491 gross tons

46m

34 m

40 m

stern

deck

Fraserburgh lifeboat station received a call to go to the assistance of any further survivors at the site of the sinking. The lifeboat *John & Charles Kennedy* put to sea and soon arrived on the scene. After surveying the area, no trace could be found of any further survivors and so, reluctantly, the *John & Charles Kennedy* returned empty-handed to its station in Fraserburgh harbour.

Against all the odds the men in the raft from the stern section were, however, still alive and well despite two freezing nights in their small open raft. They would have to suffer an even longer test of strength and character before they would be rescued. It was a staggering 36 hours before they were spotted drifting out in the open waters of the Moray Firth. Once located, a trawler was able to pluck them to safety. Although they had spent far longer adrift, ten hardy souls had survived exposure and hypothermia and the worst that could be thrown at them by the cruel sea. The death toll from *U 13*'s attack, however, was high. In total ten of the crew of the *Fram* died, including the captain and stewardess. Such personal tragedy and suffering was sadly all too common during the war and attracted only a brief comment in the local newspaper, the *Fraserburgh Herald*, on 6 February 1940 in a round-up of war events of the week.

This sinking was not the end of *U 13*'s reign of carnage at sea. On 17 April 1940 she torpedoed the 4,935-ton British steamer *Swainby* (built 1917) 25 miles north of Muckle Flugga. Eleven days later, on 28 April, she struck again, sinking the 6,999-ton British tanker *Scottish American* (built 1920) in position 58.41 00 N and 04.40 00 W. Justice, however, would be done in the end. *U 13* only continued on operations against Allied shipping for four months after sinking the *Fram*. On 31 May 1940 she was detected by the Royal Navy sloop HMS *Weston* off Lowestoft, north of Newcastle. Once the hunter, she now became the hunted. She was unable to evade her pursuers and was successfully depth-charged and sent to the bottom. This time there would be no escape for *U 13*.

Today the largest section of the wreck of the *Fram*, the stern, lies four miles directly offshore from the picturesque small fishing village of Pennan on the Aberdeenshire coast of the Moray Firth in the north-east of Scotland. Pennan recently sprang to worldwide fame as the setting for the film *Local Hero*. Its small, white fishermen's cottages nestle in practically a single row at the foot of dramatic plunging cliffs. The steep winding road down from the main coast road is not for the faint-hearted but the journey is worth while. In the summer months the one local hotel does a roaring trade serving food and drink to the many tourists who visit it. Of all the houses in Pennan only about 18 nowadays are permanent households and it is sometimes difficult to pick out a local accent amongst the small number of people browsing around the village.

The stern section of the *Fram* lies at Latitude 57 42 45 N and Longitude 02 13 22 W in 46 metres of water on a white, sandy seabed. The bow section, which is reported to have sunk almost immediately at anchor in

Aberdour Bay, has surprisingly never been located despite many echo-sounder and magnetometer searches for it. The stern section, however, drifted for 25 minutes until it sunk off Pennan, some five miles down the coast. In 1986 a local skipper reported finding a large wreck in Aberdour Bay at position 57 42 06.0 N and 02 10 32.0 W which ties in fairly closely with the original 1940 coastguard report of her anchorage position. A subsequent search by divers of this area revealed nothing but a flat, sandy seabed. Recent magnetometer searches of the Bay in the approximate area give large but confusing returns and no large section of wreck can be found with an echo-sounder. There is, however, certainly a lot of metal down there to give those magnetometer returns. I suspect that the bow section has rotted away, weakened and collapsed, so that it is not giving a discernible echo-sounder trace but is revealing its presence on the magnetometer. These readings are confused further by the fact that for many years the RAF have had a large floating target moored near the reported sinking location. For years they have been carrying out bombing exercises on this target and there are a considerable number of thunderflash shells lying on the bottom which, along with mooring chains and other debris, might give a return on the magnetometer. To add further distraction, the *Fram* is not the only vessel known to have been wrecked in Aberdour Bay.

As local divers and fishermen know, there are fairly strong tidal streams in this area. It is advisable to plan a dive on this wreck well in advance to ensure that you get slack water at neaps. It is absolutely essential to dive at slack water at spring tides. The tidal streams here are so strong that it can be very difficult just to hold on to the anchor line as you go down if you dive at the wrong time. If you get separated from the anchor line and start drifting with the current you can end up surfacing some considerable distance from the dive boat. Good surface cover and a surface marker buoy (SMB) or decompression marker are essential. There have been a number of cases reported of divers getting separated along this coastline from their surface cover and being picked up miles away downstream. If the seas have got up whilst you have been down then it can be very difficult for the surface cover to spot you when you come up if you are some way away, particularly so if they have lost sight of your bubble stream and you have no SMB. They will only know to look downstream for you. Alternatively, some other means of attracting the dive boat's attention should be carried just in case. Some divers carry personal flares and collapsable bright flags which make you easier to spot in the water if there is a difficulty. Personal flares should only be used as a last resort as you may then find yourself at the centre of a rescue if they're spotted from ashore. Remember, however, that you are diving four miles offshore and it is common to see large freighters passing between the dive boat and the land. If you get separated from your boat cover then it may be a very long time before you are picked up.

This area is also well known for sea fog which can roll in very quickly.

These factors, together with the depth of the dive, make the *Fram* a dive that is not lightly undertaken. If you want to dive the *Fram*, plan well in advance and get the tides and weather right. With careful dive planning the *Fram* will give you her best.

The underwater visibility along the stretch of north-east coastline from Buckie to Fraserburgh is one of British diving's best-kept secrets. The strong currents mean that any silt that would cloud the visibility is carried away. The seabed is swept clean, leaving only stones, boulders and clean, white sand. Visibility would be an average of 15 metres but after a few settled days in the summer it can be up to 25 metres, depending on where you are, with the stretch of water from Gardenstown to Rosehearty being perhaps the best of all. The good visibility along this stretch of water is in complete contrast to the poor, silty visibility of around 5 metres that divers encounter on the adjoining coastline that runs down the east coast from Fraserburgh down to Montrose. Many divers from the Aberdeen area make weekly pilgrimages in the summer of an hour's drive up to the Moray Firth coastline to enjoy the good visibility and rich sealife which is the hallmark of diving on this stretch of the Aberdeenshire coast.

The coastline along this stretch is made up mostly of plunging cliffs and picturesque rocky bays and inlets teeming with fulmars and puffins. The coastline is dotted with small fishing villages clustered at the foot of the cliffs, taking advantage of the shelter they provide from the prevailing north-westerly winds. The titanic forces of nature that forged this coastline have produced an underwater landscape close inshore of meandering canyons and plunging reefs. About a mile offshore, straight out from Rosehearty, is Newmill Reef which rises from a relatively flat seabed at about 30 metres up to only five metres from the surface before plunging rapidly back down to about 40 metres. Most weekends of the summer will see one or more of the local dive boats gently criss-crossing the reef with eyes fixed on an echo-sounder before anchoring up for a dive. Further out from shore the reefs and canyons end and the seabed becomes a flat, sandy boulder-field.

The strong currents mean a wealth of food for the marine filter feeders. Beyond the kelp line at about 10 to 15 metres and deeper, the seascape is quite literally covered with a carpet of sponges, dead men's fingers and anemones. The effect is that the boulders and rocks that litter the seabed appear almost white and it is only when you get in close to them that you can discern why that is. Every available foothold has been colonised. Crabs and lobsters abound, as do wrasse, cod and dogfish. It is perhaps one of the richest areas around our shores.

And so it is in fine surroundings such as this that the *Fram* has come to lie in her final resting place. Although originally anchored only about two-and-a-half miles offshore, her stern section drifted before the gale force south-easterly winds for about 30 minutes before finally slipping beneath the waves to her watery grave about four miles offshore on a flat, sandy and barren area of seabed. In this area there had previously been no real footholds for marine life to colonise but the sinking of the *Fram* changed that for ever. Away from the *Fram* the seabed is flat and sandy, littered with scallops and shells, and in places around the 50-metre mark the seabed bears tell-tale furrows marking the damage done by the ravages of the scallop dredges. The seabed is scoured as though raked by a giant comb.

Since her sinking in 1940 the *Fram* has become an oasis in an underwater desert and has now been completely colonised by marine life. She is now an artificial reef, richly covered with a carpet of sponges and anemones. Dead men's fingers abound, their brilliant white a contrast to the dark, rotting steel beneath. All sorts of fish live and die in and around the *Fram*. Wrasse hide in her nooks and crannies whilst schools of saithe drift over her decaying skeleton. Seals are often seen around the wreck, their natural curiosity sometimes getting the better of them and luring them close in. Sometimes you will look at the seabed nearby and find that the whole surface appears to be moving. At first you will think that this is just a symptom of the nitrogen nacrosis that you will inevitably be suffering from at this depth. A closer look reveals a thick cloud of fish carpeting the seabed, swaying and drifting with the current.

The *Fram* was soon forgotten about after the war; just one of the countless war losses in this area. An old vessel when she went down, her holds full of ballast rocks and in such deep water, she would not have merited any search and salvage operation. There were several rough locations for her anchoring position in Aberdour Bay although all of these varied to a large extent. The precise location of the stern section, however, was not known although doubtless many fishing boat skippers learned of its location to their cost over the years as she snagged their trawl nets. Forgotten by mankind, she was left to lie in her silent grave for 36 years until she was rediscovered in 1976 by sport divers from Aberdeen during the rapid expansion in sport diving of the 1970s. At that time the *Fram* was regarded as suitable only for hard-boat diving from a fishing boat or the like. Nowadays with the aid of the modern, fast RIB with its formidable array of electronic wreck-finding gear, it can easily be located and dived. The advent of the dry suit meant that what was formerly a deep, wetsuit dive on which the cold became a major factor can now be accomplished in warmth and comfort. On the safety side, the newer high-pressure air cylinders meant that divers could go down on her with a far greater air capacity than ever before. The world of deeper diving has been opened up by modern developments in scuba gear.

To dive the *Fram* there are really two suitable slips, one at Rosehearty to the east and the other at Gardenstown to the west. Both sites are about equidistant from the wreck site and involve a trip by RIB of about 15 minutes. Rosehearty harbour is probably the better launch site as it has recently had a new slip built which is excellent for launching and retrieving

RIBs. The car access is open and easy and the slip wide and not too steep with convenient rings set along its side. This coast is very tidal and many of the slips dry out at low water. The new slip here has been built with that in mind and boats can be launched at any state of the tide. The access to Gardenstown harbour involves an intricate drive down into the village, snaking around tight, narrow hairpins.

If you are lucky enough to have a satellite navigator on your boat then you should have no difficulty getting on to the site. For those who do not the two transits shown in the photographs are very accurate and should put you right on the site despite the distance from the shore. The wreck can then be located by echo-sounder.

The stern section of the *Fram* sits upright in 46 metres of water, lying approximately 160/340 degrees. She has divided herself into two main sections. The highest section of this wreck is the westmost end where a 20-metre long intact section, from the very stern itself forward, lies on its starboard side. The main deck slants at an angle of about 30 degrees, not far off the vertical. The beam of the *Fram* was about 14 metres and so this section, taking the angle of tilt into account, rises up from the seabed to a depth of about 35 metres. There is no evidence of any tidal scouring of the seabed around the wreck. Her four-bladed cast iron propeller still sits in place although now partially embedded in the seabed. The blades are a curious rectangular shape rather than the normal curved blade. Her large rudder still rests in its mounts, now hanging down over the rest of

Transit 1. The westmost gable en of a white house the east of Pennan and halfway up th hill shows itself around the steep headland

Transit 2. The edge of the headland to the west joins with the top of a second shelving land mass and in the distance the southern slope of a large hill

the prop. Old large-gauge fishing nets, snagged on the wreck eons ago, are draped over this section of the wreck. In places the steel of the hull has rotted away, allowing a glimpse into this towering structure.

On the steeply sloping main deck at the very stern stand the remnants of the emergency steering windlass, a T-shaped device very similar to the device found at the stern of the wreck of the *Hispania* in the Sound of Mull. Small deck hatches, their covers long gone, allow access into this section for the brave or foolhardy. A standard naval pattern emergency anchor, once shackled and resting on her deck, is now suspended beside one of these hatches with one of its flukes snagged round the hatch. Mooring bollards are dotted here and there around the edge of the deck.

Moving forward, this section of the wreck ends abruptly at a vertical drop down to the next section of the wreck. This section, the main part of the wreck, appears at an odd angle to the stern section but is in fact sitting on an even keel. The sides of the hull have rotted and collapsed, falling outwards to lie on the seabed face down, their inner ribs and spars visible, facing upwards. The main deck has collapsed downwards *en masse* and now sits squarely on the collapsed wreckage of the hull. Moving forward along this section of decking, the general depth is about 42–44 metres. The aftmost hold soon appears still quite intact externally. Looking into the hold you realise just how much the hull has collapsed as the hold has little depth. There have been many interesting finds on the *Fram* over the years, including a bicycle. Many portholes have been recovered, and recently in this hold, a ship's log, still with its glass face and dial intact, was discovered.

It was very common for steamers such as the *Fram* to carry a spare ferrous prop in case the main prop was damaged or lost a blade. Usually these spare props were situated near the stern to minimise the distance they had to be taken to be fitted in an emergency. For example, on the wreck of the *Hispania* there is a spare ferrous prop in a small hold just in front of the stern accommodation superstructure and spare props are still chained to the deck on the stern section of the *San Tiburcio*. Beside the aftmost hold on the *Fram* a large ferrous prop lies flat down in a jumble of wreckage where the deck has been opened up. The deck in places has disappeared, allowing an insight into the innards of the wreck and the prop shaft is easily visible running fore and aft through the debris.

Moving forward, a second hold appears flanked on either side by large steam-driven deck winches which would have operated a derrick system for loading and unloading the holds. None of the *Fram*'s derricks or masts remain upright now.

Further forward, the carnage caused by the torpedo strike is clearly evident. This is the start of the midships superstructure which housed the bridge, chartroom, accommodation, engine-rooms and funnel. A tangled mass of plates and collapsed square sections of superstructure reveal the force of the explosion. None of the superstructure here has survived intact. The devastated bulkheads and ribs soon give way to a more open area where there is not such a confusion of wreckage. This is the last section of the wreck and houses what was the engine-room. The *Fram* broke in two just forward of the engine-room and the blast blew off the superstructure here and opened up the engine-rooms to the sea. Drifting over this area, the steel grids of engine-room catwalks can be seen strewn here and there. A single piston is visible lying on its side near a big con rod. Towards the port rail a jumble of gearing mechanisms defy any sense of order. A heat exchanger has burst open, spilling its array of tubing. The tangle of wreckage now quickly peters out, marking the area where this section of the *Fram* was separated from the bow section during the attack.

The *Fram* lies in 46 metres of water, close to the recommended limit for air diving of 50 metres. She is a deep wreck and so everyone who dives her will inevitably suffer from nitrogen narcosis to varying degrees. The onset of the narcosis is subtle and sometimes imperceptible. Its effects on a diver's performance can, however, be dramatic and should not be underestimated. On my first dive I took down an underwater slate to sketch the wreck so that I would have some record of the dive that I could use for this chapter. Whilst down on the wreck I felt completely composed and unaffected by the narcosis as I swam over the wreck, sketching what I was seeing. Down on the wreck I thought that I had painted a virtual masterpiece. Once back ashore, however, the sketch was hardly identifiable as a ship and defied our best attempts to interpret it.

There are many reasons for including the *Fram* as one of Scotland's greatest wrecks. Her distance out from the land makes locating her without a satellite navigation system something of an art form. She is a very deep wreck, near the limits for sport diving, and is in an area affected by fierce tidal currents and where adverse sea conditions can blow up without warning. She is therefore not a dive lightly taken or for the inexperienced. The *Fram* must be treated with respect and any dive on her planned carefully, well in advance. Getting it right, however, is very rewarding. The scenery is dramatic and the coastal villages picturesque. The underwater visibility, so characteristic of this stretch of coastline, is exceptional for UK waters, rivalling the best that Scapa Flow can produce in Burra Sound and Hoxa Sound. Being so deep, however, except on the best days the *Fram* can be dark and gloomy. One of my best memories of her was on a dive on such a day. As we descended into the darkness below there was no sight of the wreck by the time we had hit 35 metres. There was another team of divers down on the wreck far away from us, one of whom was taking photos. Although it was very dark, the water clarity was so good that as his flash went off the silhouettes of large sections of the wreck flashed for an instant before our eyes before disappearing once again into the darkness. The wreck of the *Fram* itself is both scenic and yet at the same time sad. A once graceful steamer from an age gone by, blasted into two by a U-boat and consigned to the bottom for eternity.

Essential Information

Boat launch site: Rosehearty harbour or Gardenstown harbour, both 15 minutes by RIB.
Tidal conditions: Dive at slack, neaps preferably. 0–2 knots.
Visibility: 10–30 metres. 15 metres average.
Maximum depth: 46 metres.
Coastguard: Aberdeen (0224) 592334.
Police: Rosehearty (03467) 222.
Recompression chamber: National Hyperbaric Centre Ltd, 123 Ashgrove Road West, Aberdeen (0224) 698895.
Air supplies: Sub Sea Services, 631 George Street, Aberdeen (0224) 638588.
Aberdeen Watersports, 79–80 Waterloo Quay, Aberdeen (0224) 581313.
Hydrographic chart: No 222, Buckie to Fraserburgh.
Sea area: Cromarty. Tel Coastguard or Met Office for Inshore Forecast (up to five miles offshore).
Position: Lat 57 42 45.0 N, Long 02 13 22.0 W.

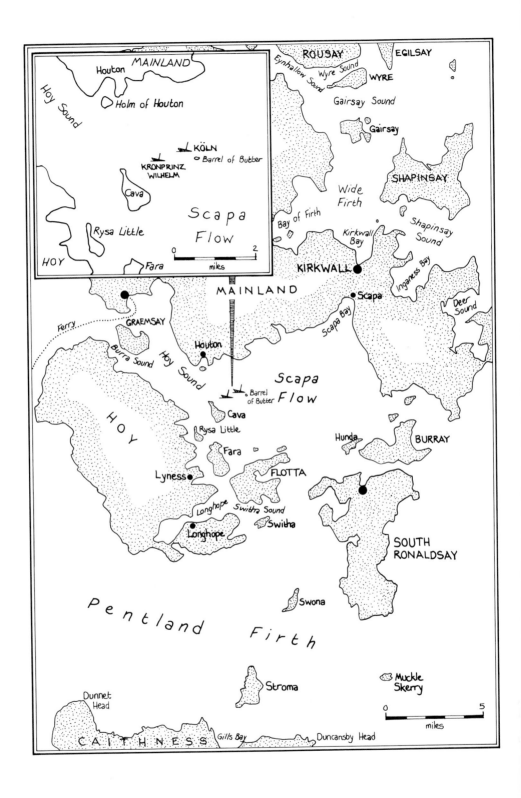

THE *KÖLN*
Scapa Flow, Orkney

When the 74 warships of the German Imperial Navy's High Seas Fleet were escorted into internment at Scapa Flow in the Orkney Islands off northern Scotland in November 1918, no one suspected how long a stay would be forced upon them. The Armistice had suspended the fighting whilst the opposing sides entered into peace negotiations which were to lead towards a lasting peace agreement: the Treaty of Versailles. During these negotiations the fleet would be interned at Scapa Flow.

The High Seas Fleet was made up of five battle-cruisers, 11 battleships, eight cruisers and 50 torpedo-boat destroyers. The Fleet ranged from the massive 656-foot long, 26,000-ton battle-cruisers *Seydlitz, Moltke, Von Der Tann, Derfflinger* and *Hindenburg*, to the smaller 24,000-ton battle-ships such as the *Kronprinz Wilhelm* and *König*, to the light cruisers of about 5,000 tons such as the *Köln* and *Dresden*, and finally to the far smaller 900-ton torpedo-boat destroyers. Once the warships had filed through the British boom defences strung across the main sea channel into the Flow they took up their internment positions in the north-west of the Flow, clustered around the islands of Cava, Hoy and Fara. The mighty battle-cruisers, battleships and light cruisers were anchored out in the deeper water of the Flow whilst the far smaller torpedo-boat destroyers could be moored in the shallower water of Gutter Sound where they could find shelter from the prevailing north-westerly winds that drive across the Flow at great strength in winter.

Once moored in position, the bulk of the 20,000 German sailors who had taken the Fleet into internment were repatriated to Germany, leaving only skeleton crews of about 200 men on the larger battle-cruisers and only 20 on destroyers. For these men internment over the winter of 1918/19 was a dismal experience. Weeks stretched into months with little progress being made in resolving the terms of the Treaty. During this time neither officers nor men were allowed to leave their ships and go ashore. The German vessels had no working radio transmitters; they had been collected and taken away by the British some time earlier. Boat traffic between ships was forbidden. The only way they could keep track with what was happening with the protracted negotiations was by reading four-day-old

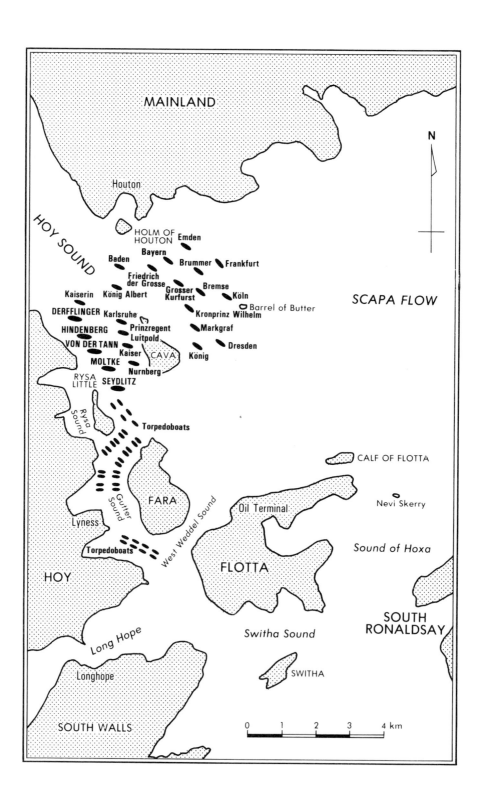

MAINLAND

Houton

HOY SOUND

HOLM OF
HOUTON   Emden
          Bayern
Baden   Brummer   Frankfurt
     Friedrich   Bremse
     der Grosse   Grosser   Köln
Kaiserin König Albert   Kurfurst
DERFFLINGER Karlsruhe   Kronprinz Wilhelm   Barrel of Butter
HINDENBERG   Prinzregent   Markgraf
VON DER TANN   Luitpold
          Kaiser   Dresden
MOLTKE   CAVA   König
RYSA   Nurnberg
LITTLE   SEYDLITZ

Rysa
Sound

          Torpedoboats

                              CALF OF FLOTTA

Gutter
Sound   Nevi Skerry

FARA   Oil Terminal

Lyness   Sound of Hoxa

          West Weddel Sound
Torpedoboats

HOY   FLOTTA   SOUTH
                          RONALDSAY

Long Hope   Switha Sound

Longhope   SWITHA

SOUTH WALLS

SCAPA FLOW

N

0   1   2   3   4 km

newspapers. The old newspapers were avidly read by the German crews and what they learned was supplemented by word-of-mouth reports from the crews of resupply vessels that came regularly from Germany to replenish the Fleet. The Allies had insisted at the very beginning of the Armistice talks that the Germans would have to be responsible for supplying their own Fleet whilst it was in internment. They were provided only with water, coal and oil. The British recognised the insurmountable difficulties that would be caused in supplying these necessities from Germany for the entire Fleet of 74 vessels. Everything else, including food, had to be sent from Germany. Generally the health of the interned crews did not suffer too badly. The biggest problem proved to be the state of the men's teeth for there was not a single dentist in the Fleet and the British were not prepared to allow access to dental facilities ashore.

The Fleet lay motionless at anchor for seven long months as the peace negotiations dragged on without any end in sight. The once-proud mighty ships of the High Seas Fleet slowly became covered with surface rust as the months of internment passed. Although disarmed and impotent, the Fleet dominated the skyline of the Flow, dwarfing the British patrol boats and tenders that moved around in amongst these mighty vessels. Elements of the British Grand Fleet detailed to guard the High Seas Fleet were moored in the Flow close by.

As dawn broke on the morning of 21 June 1919 the early shafts of sunlight filtering over the horizon threw off the mantle of darkness that had lain over the ships. The crews started to rouse themselves and go about their daily duties, most unaware of the dramatic events that would unfold that day. For some it would be an end to their enforced and confined stay aboard the moored vessels. For other less fortunate souls 21 June 1919 would be the day they died.

During their internment the German sailors had studied newspapers that the British passed to them, trying to follow the progress of the peace negotiations. The British thought that the Germans could learn little from them that would be of assistance to them but they were to be proved tragically wrong in this belief. Rear Admiral Ludwig von Reuter, the officer in charge of the German Fleet, had been carefully following the peace negotiations in these old newspapers. In the days leading up to 21 June he had read, with increasing anxiety, how the peace negotiations appeared to be breaking down. Germany would not comply with the Allied demands and both sides started to adopt more aggressive attitudes towards each other. If the Armistice broke down then the dogs of war would be unleashed again. Reuter suspected that if the fighting started again then the British would immediately board and seize the disabled High Seas Fleet. Disarmed and manned only by skeleton crews, the Germans could not have resisted a storming by well-armed British marines. The only way he could prevent his valuable Fleet falling into British hands would be by scuttling the entire Fleet. On 17 June he issued coded contingency orders to the commanders of the ships in the Fleet to cover

Opposite: Mooring positions of the High Seas Fleet

The High Seas Fleet at anchor from Houton Bay

such an eventuality. Reuter's trusted sailors opened all doors and hatches, fixing them in position to enable the vessels to flood more easily. Seacocks were set on a hair turning and lubricated thoroughly. Large hammers were placed beside any valves which, when smashed, would allow seawater to flood in. Sea valves were opened and disconnected from the upper decks to prevent any British boarding party from slowing the flood of water into the vessels from the decks above. Bulkhead rivets were prised out and seawater pipes were made ready for smashing. Finally all the preparations were ready. The commanders of the individual vessels simply awaited the coded order to scuttle and for security reasons the plan was kept secret from the crews.

From a four-day-old newspaper Reuter learned that the Armistice was to have ended on 21 June and thus the fighting would recommence if actual peace terms could not be agreed. Reading the reports of the stances being taken by either side, Reuter concluded that no agreement to continue the Armistice seemed probable. In fact the two sides had agreed to extend the Armistice by two days to seven p.m. on Monday 23 June. Reuter later claimed to have been unaware of this although the British always maintained that he had been informed. In any event he resolved to scuttle the Fleet on 21 June.

As Reuter roused himself that morning and looked out from his flagship, the cruiser *Emden*, he saw that it was a fine, clear summer's day. The sky above was a deep blue and the water of the Flow only slightly choppy. He dressed himself slowly in his full dress uniform with the insignia of his highest decorations around his neck. The Iron Cross and his other medals were pinned to the breast of his frock-coat.

At ten a.m. Reuter went out on to the *Emden*'s quarter-deck. One of his officers approached him immediately, saluted and spoke with him for a short period. The hand of fate had dealt Reuter an ace and he could hardly believe his luck. At nine a.m. that very morning the British guard fleet, the First Battle Squadron commanded by Sir Sydney Fremantle and made up of five battleships, two light cruisers and nine destroyers, had left the Flow for the first time in the seven months of internment to carry out a torpedo-firing exercise at sea. A small guard force of three British destroyers, *Vegar*, *Vesper* and the unserviceable *Victorious*, had been left behind to watch over the 74 German vessels. The First Battle Squadron was under orders to be back in the Flow by the new expiry date for the Armistice, 23 June, in case of any trouble.

Reuter ordered that the international code flags 'DG' be raised on the *Emden*. This signal alerted the commanders of the other vessels in the Fleet that they were to man their bridges and keep a special lookout for further signals.

At 10.30 a.m. Reuter addressed an attendant signaller and shortly afterwards a string of command flags appeared above the *Emden* despite it being outwith the times the British permitted for signalling. The order read 'Paragraph 11. Bestätigen' (Paragraph eleven. Confirm). Reuter had given the momentous prearranged coded order to his commanders to scuttle their vessels. The signal to scuttle was repeated from ship to ship by semaphore and by Morse code on signal lamps, a slow process when 74 ships had to receive the order. The southernmost ships of the long lines of destroyers were not visible from the *Emden* and had to wait for a full hour for the signal to reach them. Slowly, one by one, the prearranged formal responses came back to the *Emden*. The first response was received at 11.30 a.m. just as the original signal to scuttle reached the last of the destroyers: 'Paragraph eleven is confirmed'. In a patriotic gesture of defiance many of the German ships ran up the Imperial Navy ensign at their sterns. They had been forbidden by the Allies from displaying the striking white flag with its bold black cross and eagle. The flag had not been seen before at Scapa Flow. Others ran up the red flag, the letter 'Z' which in international code signalled 'Advance on the enemy'.

At first after the scuttling had started nothing seemed to happen. From above the surface nothing seemed obviously wrong to the eye. Below decks, however, tons of cold, green seaweater was flooding into the vessels. Soon the weight of inrushing water would alter the trim of the vessels. By then it would be too late for the British to stop the scuttling.

At around noon an artist out aboard a British Navy trawler to sketch

the German Fleet at anchor noticed that small boats were being lowered down the side of some of the German vessels against British standing orders and alerted a British officer. Sixteen minutes later the first of the German Fleet to sink, the 24,380-ton battleship *Friedrich Der Grosse*, turned turtle and went to the bottom.

As time passed all of the ships started to assume increasingly strange tilts and angles as the weight of water altered their buoyancy and trim. Some of the great vessels rolled slowly on to their sides while others went down by the stern or bow, forcing the other end of the vessel to lift high out of the water. Others settled on an even keel. Those that had been moored in shallow water settled on the seabed with their superstructure, masts and funnels showing clear of the water. As the cold seawater reached the engine-rooms of the vessels, blasts of steam, oil and air roared out of the ships' vents and white clouds of steam billowed upwards.

As each vessel passed from sight a whirlpool was created. Debris swirled around in it, slowly being sucked inwards and eventually, relentlessly, being pulled into the murky depths. Gradually oil escaped from the submerged ships, bursting on the surface in a kaleidoscope of colour and then spreading outwards to cover the surface of the Flow with a dark film. Scattered across the Flow was the debris that the vessels' passing from sight had left. The Flow was littered with empty boats rocking in the calm waters, lifebelts, spars and other debris. German sailors lined up on the deck of one vessel to cheer a farewell to another ship close by as it slipped beneath the waves. On the deck of the *Baden* a German sailor was seen to dance a hornpipe.

The 5,531-ton light cruiser *Köln* had been moored a few hundred yards north of the rocky outcrop in the middle of the Flow called the Barrel of Butter. She lay not far from Reuter's flagship *Emden*, itself moored near Holm of Houton to the north. The *Köln* was one of the first vessels to get the order to scuttle. Soon her seawater valves and seacocks were open and their keys and handles thrown overboard. Seawater pipes were smashed and condensers opened. The flood of water into her hull was uncontrollable and unstoppable. The *Köln* settled deeper and deeper into the waters of the Flow as her skeleton crew abandoned ship in an open cutter. The light cruiser *Brummer* had been moored nearby and her crew in another open cutter closed to join company with the crew of the *Köln*. Sailors on a British drifter nearby sent small-arms warning shots spraying into the water around the cutters, forcing them to part in an effort to drive the crews back aboard their vessels. Kapitan Leutnant Heinemann in charge of the *Köln* ordered his men to take off their caps so that they could not be identified from the name on the ribbon and so put back on their ship.

A British destroyer came alongside the *Köln* in an attempt to board her or take her in tow to shallow water, an attempt that would nearly have tragic consequences. The bow of the *Köln* lifted slowly. The water was now almost level with her main deck; she was not long for this world.

Gracefully she went down by the stern, rolling slowly on to her starboard side and only narrowly missing the British destroyer.

The *Köln* finally slipped beneath the waves at Scapa Flow at 1.50 p.m., some two-and-a-half hours after the order to scuttle had been issued by Reuter. When the news of the scuttling got out to Fremantle and the First Battle Squadron on exercise he immediately ordered his Squadron to return to the Flow at full speed. The fastest of the British ships were able to get back to the Flow by two p.m. As they charged into the Flow at 22 knots, smashing through the short seas of the Flow, they may have just caught sight of the *Köln* as it went under. The last of the First Battle Squadron would not arrive in the Flow until four p.m. by which time only three German battleships, three light cruisers and a few destroyers would be afloat out of the 74 warships of the German High Seas Fleet.

The *Köln* had been moored in deep water of 35 metres and the plunge down from the surface to the seabed below would have taken 20 to 30 seconds. With all the air displaced from her hull by water the *Köln* would have almost regained an even keel as she sank, picking up speed as her plunge to the seabed continued. As she impacted on to the soft seabed a huge explosion of silt brought clouds of mud billowing up from the seabed. The *Köln* rolled slowly over on to her starboard side and settled in her watery grave, still at last. For some time the clouds of silt disturbed

The light cruiser *Köln* (Courtesy Imperial War Museum)

146

by her impact on the seabed rained down on her, covering her in a fine film of silt. The *Köln* had finally come to rest on the bottom of Scapa Flow.

On the surface far above, her crew remained in the open cutter, watching their home for the last seven months passing into history. Once she had gone the cutter was taken in tow by a British drifter and the crew placed under arrest aboard Fremantle's flagship HMS *Revenge*, eventually being repatriated to Germany.

Over the coming decades the majority of the scuttled German Fleet was raised from the deep in the greatest feat of marine salvage ever seen. The *Köln* and six other of the High Seas Fleet, however, would never be torn from their deep water graves and broken down for scrap. Today in the cold, dark waters of Scapa Flow the *Köln* lies with her sister light cruisers *Dresden*, *Brummer* and *Karlsruhe*, and the 26,000-ton battleships *Kronprinz Wilhelm*, *Markgraf* and *König*.

The 5,531-ton light cruiser *Köln* was built in Hamburg by Blohm & Voss. Although she was launched on 5 October 1916 she did not join the High Seas Fleet until January 1918. The *Köln* was a sleek, fast and manoeuvrable vessel, 510 feet in length, with a beam of 47 feet and a draught of 21 feet. She was powered by two sets of coal/oil-fired turbines and twin propellers which could push her to speeds of more than 29 knots.

The *Köln* was both well armed and well protected. She boasted 2.4-inch main belt and deck armour. Her control tower, the nerve centre of the ship, was protected by thicker 3.9-inch armour. She had eight 5.9-inch guns set in single turrets. Two were mounted side by side on the foredeck, near the bow, able to rotate 180 degrees and fire out over either side of the ship. Two further turrets were situated on either side of the bridge. These turrets again were able to rotate 180 degrees and thus allow the gun to be trained from dead ahead to dead astern. Two further 5.9-inch guns were mounted one either side of the mainmast (aftmost mast). These were trained aft, capable of firing from dead astern to almost dead ahead. The final two turrets were situated at the stern trained dead astern. One was situated on the main deck and the other, just above and forward of it, on the superstructure deck. Both these guns could rotate forward to either the port or starboard sides of the ship until they were trained forward just 38 degrees off the centre line. Six guns could be brought to bear in a broadside with each shell weighing 46 kg.

The *Köln* also boasted two 3.4-inch high elevation guns set in single mountings on the centre line of the ship, located near the stern between the mainmast and the after funnel. These smaller rapid-firing guns could fire ten 9.5-kg shells per minute and were able to rotate through a full 360 degrees. They were capable of elevating to 80 degrees or of lowering to ten degrees below the horizontal to target vessels close to the ship.

Four 23.6-inch deck mounted torpedo tubes and 200 mines completed her armoury. One torpedo tube was situated either side of the foremast

The wreck of the
light cruiser *Köln*

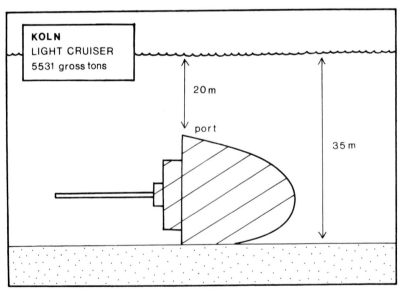

and one either side of the aftermost funnel. These tubes were far more versatile than the previous underwater tubes and could be aimed over a wide angle from 140 to 90 degrees.

The *Köln*'s heavily armoured control or conning tower was built into the bridge superstructure. Shielded by 3.9-inch armour, it had thin viewing slits ranged round its oval frontage on two deck levels. On top of the conning tower sat the optical rangefinder for the guns, well away from spray and cordite smoke. On both the foremast and mainmast there were searchlight platforms and far above them the spotting top.

The crew's accommodation and mess rooms were located at the bow of the *Köln* in the two deck levels directly underneath the two side-by-side 5.9-inch guns. The officers' accommodation was located in the superstructure deck at the stern of the vessel directly underneath the aft superimposed 5.9-inch gun turret. It was entered by a heavy-hinged doorway and the accommodation bulkheads were lined with square windows unlike the crews' accommodation which only had the usual portholes. Her full ship's complement comprised 559 officers and men.

The wreck of the mighty light cruiser *Köln* now lies in 35 metres of water at position 58 53 32 N and 03 08 27 W not far from the rocky outcrop in the middle of the Flow known as the Barrel of Butter. This is used as a haul-out site by a large population of grey seals which can be seen basking in the sun on summer days. If you approach in a dive boat they all take to the water, their own environment where they are far safer. Scores of dark heads bob out of the water, keeping a watchful eye on the perceived threat and disappearing in a splash of water if they sense real danger.

The *Köln* lies on her starboard side well settled into the silty bottom. The entire Fleet was anchored in a WNW direction and the *Köln* settled with that same bearing. The least depth over her upward-facing port side is about 20 metres. There is so much to see on the *Köln* and she is in such good condition that she is rightly regarded as one of the finest dives in the Flow. Barring the removal of her propellers, salvaged long ago, and some salvage blasting in her engine-room area near the stern, she is relatively much the same as the day she went down.

Diving the *Köln* gives a real impression of deep-water diving from a hard boat. From Stromness or Burray it is about an hour's steaming until the dive boat arrives over the site, time enough to get your gear sorted out and get kitted up. By the time you get on site you will feel that you are miles from land with a lot of deep, dark water beneath you.

The *Köln* is usually marked by a small buoy moored just aft of the bridge, a source of fascination if you haven't dived her before. Once on site, however, if you want to dive a different part of the wreck your skipper will drop a weighted shot line. The skippers know the Scapa wrecks so well that they will be able to drop their shot practically on any area of the wreck that you want. The *Köln* is a substantial vessel and 510 feet in length is a lot of swimming if you want to see the whole wreck. If you are doing a repeat dive on her you may want to be dropped on the stern section to see the two 5.9-inch gun turrets, officers' accommodation or the mainmast and its platforms. Your skipper should be able to drop his shot right on to that area to allow you to spend some time here. At this depth your bottom time is short enough anyway without having to swim the entire length of the wreck to get to the area you really want to explore.

Once the shot is down on the correct area of the wreck it is time for the dive briefing. This is a deep dive and it is essential that everyone knows the depth they will be going to, the maximum time they can stay down on the wreck, the layout of the wreck and the main features they can expect to see on the dive. Once the dive briefing is over the divers split up into their buddy pairs and finish kitting up. Hoods are pulled on and masks cleared and made ready. Air bottles are hoisted on and weight belts carefully positioned and tightened. The divers carry out their buddy checks, making sure that their buddy diver's gear is all in working order. Finally they are ready and the skipper closes on the shot line to drop the divers. There is little current for the divers to worry about in this part of the Flow.

One by one the divers take a deep breath and then leap from the safety of the dive boat, their hearts racing as they drop the six feet or so down into the water. Their vision is filled with a mass of white bubbles as they splash into the water and then bob back up to the surface. Once both buddy divers are in the water they can head for the shot line which they will follow down into the black depths below. The wreck is far below, well out of sight. The shot line seems to plunge directly down into a black, inky void, disappearing into the darkness below. The divers will use the shot as a guideline down into the depths to ensure that they don't drift away from the wreck as they descend. In deep water like this there is always a midway point on the descent when the divers cannot see the surface above them or the wreck below. This can be an uneasy and unsettling feeling for the inexperienced diver. Drifting weightless in such an environment it is easy for the diver to become disoriented and lose his sense of direction. If there is a slight current running, then without a shot line the divers could well find themselves missing the wreck and landing on a soft, silty seabed at 35 metres with no sign of the wreck.

The visibility in this part of the Flow is an average of 10–15 metres and so the divers can see each other clearly as they descend and can see other groups of divers above and below them. The divers' eyes strain into the gloom beneath, searching for their first sight of one of the famous survivors from the legendary High Seas Fleet. As the distance from the surface increases the natural light filtering down decreases but the divers' eyes soon adjust to the change. Slowly the port side of the hull of the *Köln* seems to materialise out of the gloom. At first sight it looks just like the seabed, covered in grey/brown silt and sponges and anemones. Unlike the seabed, which is soft and yielding, when you land on the hull you soon find that beneath the covering of silt there is a solid and immovable mass of best German armour plating. Rows of portholes stretch in lines along the hull, allowing a glimpse into the black and foreboding interior of the vessel. The hull slopes away downwards to its keel on one side and runs off in the other direction until it stops at a seemingly vertical cliff. This is the edge of the now vertical deck. As the divers reach the edge they can peer down the wood-planked deck, its timbers still clearly visible despite more than 70 years immersion in the sea. Although as the divers descended from the surface they were aware of their surroundings getting darker and darker, now, looking over the edge, it seems at first to be pitch black beneath. The *Köln* is so large that it casts a considerable shadow, blocking out any sunlight that would normally reach down to her deck.

The divers have arrived at the bow and after a further check on their buddy they can fin out over the black void beneath and descend slowly down the vertical deck. The pointed bow, designed to slice at speed through the water, runs off to their right as they start finning aft. Almost immediately they come upon anchor hawsepipes and mooring bollards set at the edge of the deck. The two forward anchor chains which would have held the vessel in place as it scuttled are still run out from their chain lockers to two large and distinctive, circular, steam-driven capstans, some five feet in diameter, which jut out vertically from the deck. One of the anchor chains, each link the size of a man's hand, loops up in a dramatic arc to the port hawsepipe before plunging down vertically to the seabed 10 metres below and running out along it for some distance.

Both side-by-side 5.9-inch bow gun turrets which would have been located just aft of the anchor capstans have been salvaged in the past, leaving only the remnants of their wracking systems embedded in the deck. In this area there are several large openings in the deck that allow divers to see into the cavernous hull spaces in the deck level immediately beneath the main deck.

The bridge superstructure looms out of the gloom, blocking the divers path aft. Immediately in front of the main superstructure sits the control or conning tower. This solid oval structure, two deck levels high, was the nerve centre of the vessel and was heavily protected with 3.9-inch armour plating. To minimise its vulnerability under fire there were no windows as such. Officers were able to peer out through thin one-inch-high viewing slits ranged around the tower on two levels, one directly above the other. Situated on top of the tower can be found the optical central gun-control rangefinder. Sighting periscopes were also situated here but these have been removed, leaving holes which allow divers to peer inside the tower. It is heavily filled with silt and pendulous rivulets of rust hang down from any available foothold. The tower can no longer be entered through its original door because of the way the ship is lying. The *Köln* was the first German light cruiser to have its fire control tower built within the bridge superstructure. Previously the tower had been situated separately, some distance forward of the bridge (as with the *Brummer*). The *Köln*'s revolutionary set-up meant that the control tower was higher than its predecessors. Today the *Köln*'s control tower still seems to be situated separately from the bridge superstructure but part of the bridge superstructure has either rusted away or been removed to leave the control tower exposed and seemingly separate from the bridge superstructure.

Immediately aft of the control tower the open command bridge superstructure juts far out from the deck. The foremast rises through the superstructure and runs off down to the seabed, some of its cross rigging still in place, now well encrusted with sealife. The two searchlight platforms are still *in situ* although the lights themselves are long gone. Set in the wood-lined deck just aft of the superstructure and towards the port side of the hull is an open companionway hatch that once would have led down into the bowels of the ship. It is now partly filled with silt, blocking access. The ladder with its brass treads is still in place, emerging from the silt near the hatch itself. The *Köln* had three funnels but these have now rusted and broken off, falling down to litter the seabed below. Cavernous black holes with torn remnants of the funnels themselves mark where they stood. On the topmost port side of the hull, empty lifeboat davits hang outwards, their boats having been lowered as the crew made good their escape during the scuttling.

Moving further aft, the silhouette of the mainmast materialises out of the gloom. It runs off down to the seabed at an unnatural angle. The cause is soon apparent. A large hole some 10 metres across has been blasted here by salvors attempting to open up the hull to recover the precious non-ferrous metal from the engine-rooms located immediately beneath the mainmast. The large, circular, secondary gun director platform with two searchlight platforms above can still be located on the mainmast. Immediately above on the edge of the port side of the hull can be found a 5.9-inch gun, its barrel pointing upwards at an angle towards the distant surface. The raised decking on which the gun turret once stood has corroded away, revealing the cylindrical housing for the turret's turning mechanism.

The blasted hole has destroyed the structural integrity of the vessel in this area. The hull has been opened up from the upmost port side right down to the seabed. Exploring in here gives an insight into the innards of the light cruiser. The far side of the blasted area where the hull resumes a ship shape appears blurred in the distance, at the limit of the underwater visibility here. Just beyond this hole lies the officers' accommodation. This superstructure has a row of square windows set in it, the glass long gone. In the middle of this row there is a large hinged doorway, the door open and lying on the bulkhead. This doorway gives access into the innards of the *Köln* but divers should not consider penetrating the hull unless they are experienced in wreck penetration diving, know exactly where and what they are going to see and are properly equipped with lights, ropes and reels. It is all too easy in these dark hulls to become disoriented and lose the way out. Careless finning in these enclosed spaces sends clouds of silt billowing up from the bottom, instantly blotting out the visibility.

Situated on top of this deck-house sits the after superimposed 5.9-inch gun turret, its barrel still locked in position pointing dead astern as it had done throughout the long months of internment and the dramatic scuttling itself. Its barrel, breech and firing mechanism remain in relatively good condition, now encrusted with sealife. The long, heavy barrel juts out over the bulkhead marking the end of the deck-house. Immediately beneath on the quarter-deck sits the aftmost 5.9-inch gun turret, its barrel also pointing dead astern. The barrel points out over the single circular steam-driven anchor capstan. The Fleet generally were only moored by their forward anchors during internment, moving around with the prevailing wind and seas. The stern anchor itself was not run out at the time of the scuttling and still sits neatly in its hawse. Finally the very stern of the *Köln* itself is reached, its rounded edge dotted with mooring bollards and on the hull itself, rows of portholes. The heavy rudder lies flat on the seabed, its two valuable propellers long gone, the subject of some of the first small-scale salvaging that has taken place on this mighty wreck.

Essential Information

Boat launch site: For RIBS, Houton Bay, Stromness harbour, Scapa pier or Burray. Otherwise dive by hard boat.
Tidal conditions: $0-\frac{1}{2}$ knot maximum. Dive at any state of the tide.
Visibility: 10–20 metres average.
Maximum depth: Seabed 35 metres, least depth over port side of hull, 20 metres.
Coastguard: Kirkwall (0856) 873268.
Police: Stromness (0856) 850222.
Air supplies: All the hard boats have onboard compressors.
Sea area: Fair Isle.
Recompression chamber: National Hyperbaric Centre Ltd, 123 Ashgrove Road West, Aberdeen (0224) 698895.
Hydrographic chart: No 35, Scapa Flow & Approaches.
Position: Lat 58 53 32 N, Long 03 08 27 W.

THE
KRONPRINZ WILHELM
Scapa Flow, Orkney

World War I, the Great War, was the most savage and bitter war that the world had ever seen. For five long, dismal years the world had been locked in a bloody and brutal conflict. On land troops struggled to live in the squalid, rat-infested trenches of the European battlefield and were slaughtered in their thousands in the stalemate of trench warfare. Countless battles were fought that still live on in man's memory; the Somme, Ypres and many others, each a testament to the bravery of mankind.

In the years leading up to the war, Britain and Germany had become locked in an arms race that had led to the creation of a new breed of warship; the dreadnought. As each side struggled for naval supremacy, the emergence of the dreadnoughts revolutionised naval warfare. Virtually overnight the old warships, the pre-dreadnoughts, were rendered obsolete. The Royal Navy had for centuries gauged its strength by the famous 'two power standard'. The philosophy behind this standard was that the Royal Navy must always be equal in strength to the combined sea power of the second and third largest navies in the world. At the end of the 19th century Kaiser Wilhelm II and the then Captain Alfred von Tirpitz dreamed of ending Britain's naval supremacy and of winning control of the seas. Together they masterminded a huge German naval arms build-up. This caused much concern to the British Admiralty who had to match it if they were to stick to the much revered two power standard. So began a momentous arms race as both sides frantically armed for the hostilities that each side knew were inevitable.

In 1906 Britain got the breakthrough it needed with the revolutionary construction of HMS *Dreadnought*. She was so far ahead of her time that she gave her name to the new breed of ship. The new dreadnoughts were about ten per cent bigger than their predecessors and at £1.75 million (in 1905), much more expensive. They were faster and had thicker armour and greater fire-power. Each had ten 12-inch guns that could hurl 850-lb shells about 18,500 yards. Three of the five gun turrets were centred on the middle line of the vessel with one gun turret on either side amidships. The dreadnought, unlike its predecessors, could therefore fire a broadside of eight shells to either side, six ahead and two astern. For the first time all eight guns, which were previously fired independently, could be aimed and fired in unison by one gunnery officer. One dreadnought could match two pre-dreadnoughts for fire-power at long range and three when firing ahead.

Originally known simply as the *Kronprinz*, the *Kronprinz Wilhelm* was renamed on 27 January 1918 in honour of Kaiser Wilhelm II on his 59th birthday. She was a fine example of this new breed of dreadnought. Built by Germaniawerft in Kiel and launched on 21 February 1914, she and her sister dreadnoughts *Markgraf* and *König* were so large that the Kiel Canal had to be specially widened to allow them to pass through it after their completion. Her specifications were awesome indeed. She displaced 25,388 tons and was 575 feet long with a beam of 97 feet and a draught of over 30 feet. Her main armour belt was a staggering 13.8 inches thick. Her vital areas such as her gun turrets and control tower were shielded by 11.8-inch armour plating, her deck by 3.9-inch armour plating. Powered by three coal/oil-fired turbines that generated 46,000 horsepower, she was the fastest dreadnought in her class. Her three great propellers could drive her at speeds of up to 21.3 knots.

The *Kronprinz* bristled with firepower. Ten 12-inch guns, set in five twin turrets made up her main armament. Her secondary armament was made up of fourteen 5.9-inch casemate guns ranged along her battery deck. Each was set on its own rotating pedestal with the barrels effectively protruding from the hull side. Each casemate gun was protected by a 6.75-inch thick steel turret front which rotated with the gun. These guns could hurl seven 101-lb shells per minute over a distance of eight miles and were used to attack smaller craft such as torpedo-boat destroyers which would try to close for a broadside shot at a battleship. Like the main armament these casemate guns could be aimed remotely from the fire control tower. Added to this arsenal were two 3.45-inch anti-aircraft guns and five submerged torpedo tubes, one to the bow and four in the beam.

The *Kronprinz* was manned by a crew of 1,136 men and was effectively a floating village with five deck levels in the hull space alone, communicating principally by voice pipes. Underneath the casemate deck was the middle deck where the officers' and crew's mess spaces were located. The crew's accommodation was also located here and as an innovation was centrally heated by the boilers below, the temperature being kept at 50 degrees Farenheit. The officer's accommodation was situated aft on two levels with the captain and other senior officers having additional cabins on and below the bridge. The officers' accommodation was kept warmer than the crew's at 58 degrees Farenheit. Below this lay the armoured deck housing coal bunkers, storerooms and engineers' workshops. Beneath the armoured deck, below the waterline, lay the upper platform deck, housing the shell rooms, anchor capstan motors and the steering machinery for the twin rudders. The lower platform deck below housed four torpedo rooms, fresh water tanks and the magazines containing the cordite shell propellant. The boilers, turbines, propeller

The *König* class battleship *Kronprinz Wilhelm* (Imperial War Museum)

shaft and gyro compass rooms were a further deck down. Below this lay the ship's double bottom which had areas for storing oil and fresh water.

The German High Seas Fleet was thus constructed at enormous cost and had to be maintained at a similarly high cost throughout the war. It was so highly prized by the Kaiser that during the course of the war he never dared to risk it in an all-out confrontation with the mighty Royal Navy. To suffer a crippling defeat at the hands of the Royal Navy would give the British undisputed mastery of the seas. The Royal Navy, however, were eager for just such a confrontation and would finally catch up with the German High Seas Fleet for the one momentous sea battle of World War I; the Battle of Jutland.

Admiralty intelligence had learned that elements of the German High Seas Fleet were about to leave port on a raiding mission and so the British Grand Fleet was ordered out to sea to carry out a sweep across the northern sector of the North Sea towards the expanse of water known by the Germans as the Skagerrak, which leads into the *Kattegat* channel between Denmark and Norway. It was 30 May 1916.

The British Battle Fleet, commanded by Admiral Sir John Jellicoe, left Scapa Flow with its 24 battleships, three battle-cruisers, escort destroyers and scout cruisers to rendezvous with the Battle-cruiser Fleet led by Vice-Admiral Sir David Beatty. He had set out from Rosyth in the Firth of

Forth with six battle-cruisers, four battleships, destroyers and scout ships. The British Battle-cruiser Fleet, on its way from Rosyth to the rendezvous and the German Scouting Group of the High Seas Fleet, commanded by Vice Admiral Hipper, had moved by chance into relatively close proximity of each other although neither knew the whereabouts of the other. The German force was made up of five battle-cruisers, four light cruisers and attendant destroyer screens. The main part of the German Fleet lay some 50 miles to the south. By the afternoon of 31 May the two fleets were steaming on almost parallel courses, each out of sight of the other over the horizon, about 20 miles apart. The hand of fate decreed that an unsuspecting neutral Danish steamer, the *N.J. Fjord*, would steam unwittingly in between the two fleets, visible to both sides. The German Scouting Group sent the torpedo boats *B109* and *B110* over to carry out a routine search. The British light cruiser *Galatea*, scouting on the edge of the Beatty's Battle-cruiser Fleet, changed course to do the same and the die was cast. The *Galatea* saw the smoke of the departing German torpedo boats who in turn saw the *Galatea*'s approach and suddenly both sides were aware of each other's presence.

Battle commenced at about 2.20 p.m. and raged throughout that afternoon as the two opposing lines of dreadnoughts, each some eight miles long, wheeled and tried to out-manoeuvre each other for position. At first Hipper turned to run to the south, leading the pursuing British Force towards the main element of the German Fleet. At 4.05 p.m. a series of salvoes from the 18,700-ton battle-cruiser *Von Der Tann* struck the last ship in the British line, HMS *Indefatigable* which was destroyed in a cataclysmic magazine explosion in which 1,015 men were killed. The 26,000-ton battle-cruiser HMS *Queen Mary* was targeted by the mighty guns of *Derfflinger* and *Seydlitz* and in a hail of fire exploded and sank quickly. Only eight of a crew of 1,274 survived.

The British cruiser *Southampton* was sent to scout some way ahead of the battle and reported to Beatty that it was not simply a force of German battle-cruisers that had been engaged but in fact the full High Seas Fleet. Six divisions of the German Battle Fleet, 16 battleships and six pre-dreadnoughts were steaming at full speed towards the action. Beatty then changed tactics to lure the German Fleet northwards towards the mighty guns of the battleships that formed Jellicoe's Battle Fleet on its way to the rendezvous from Scapa Flow. Beatty wheeled his ships to the south to let the Germans catch full sight of them and then altered course to run northwards in front of the German Fleet, luring the High Seas Fleet closing for the kill towards Jellicoe's guns. This manoeuvre took the British rearguard ships *Malaya* and *Warspite* within the range of the guns of the German vanguard, the Third Battleship Squadron, resulting in a furious exchange of fire. At the front of the German vanguard was the mighty battleship *König*. Fourth in the line of seven battleships was the *Kronprinz Wilhelm* which kept up a murderous hail of fire on the British vessels. The *Malaya* and *Warspite* were hit many times and took heavy casualties, many of whom now lie in the naval cemetery at Lyness on the island of Hoy.

The British ships could make 24 knots whilst the German ships could only make 23 knots. Eventually, this superior British speed took their vessels beyond the range of the German guns and from this safe distance the British ships with their superior range could keep up a hail of fire on the German pursuers as they led them into a well-rehearsed trap.

The chase lasted for more than an hour before the reality of the situation dawned on the Germans. The German vanguard ships were confronted by Jellicoe's Battle Fleet in line astern stretching along the horizon from north-east to north-west for as far as the Germans could see. The British had successfully accomplished the classic naval manoeuvre of 'crossing the T'. The British battleships were able to fire repeated broadsides at the German line whilst only the lead German vessel could return fire. Salvo after salvo of shells rained down on the German lead ships as the trap was sprung. The *König* at the very front of the German line was badly hit many times and soon took on a four-and-a-half degree list. The *Lützow*, the flagship of the battle-cruiser force, already damaged from the earlier action, was fatally wounded and withdrew and sank shortly after.

Quickly the Germans tried to escape from the cauldron of death they had been lured into. The whole Fleet was turned around to flee to the south. The huge billowing clouds of smoke created by the dreadnoughts' engines and guns caused both fleets to lose sight of each other and destroyed the effectiveness of the barrage. In a gap in the smoke *Derfflinger* sighted the battle-cruiser HMS *Invincible*, silhouetted on the northern horizon 10,000 yards away, well in range of her powerful guns. The *Invincible* was fatally struck, breaking in two.

In the confusion of the smoke Admiral Scheer turned his fleet to the east but still they were pounded by the fierce British guns. Some German ships turned away without waiting for orders, causing others to stop or take evasive action to avoid collisions. Admiral Behncke saved the day for the Germans by turning *König* into the wind and effectively creating a smokescreen which would cover the German withdrawal. Simultaneously German torpedo boats attacked the British battleships. The smoke from their stacks added to the cover and their torpedoes darting through the water caused the British battleships to take evasive action. In the confusion caused by this counter-attack the main German Fleet was able to disappear from sight in the smoke and fading light.

Skirmishing between the fleets continued after darkness with the last shots being fired at about 3.20 a.m. The battle had lasted for 13 hours during which the German High Seas Fleet had lost one pre-dreadnought battleship and one battle-cruiser. Two thousand, five hundred and fifty-one German sailors were killed and 507 wounded.

The British Grand Fleet came off numerically worse with the loss of three battle-cruisers, three cruisers, one light cruiser and seven destroyers.

Six thousand and ninety-seven British servicemen were killed in action, 510 were wounded and 177 taken prisoner by the Germans. The statistics do not take account, however, of the far higher ratio of damaged ships on the German side. The Royal Navy retained undisputed mastery of the seas and the German High Seas Fleet was deterred from taking any further large-scale action against the British as a result.

The *Kronprinz* came through that epic clash unscathed, with no casualties despite being in the thick of the fighting and raining a murderous hail of fire on to the British warships. Apart from this crucial battle, the *Kronprinz*, although involved in many missions, saw action on only one other occasion. She would not be so lucky this time. At 10.30 p.m. on 4 November 1916 Admiral Hipper led the *Kronprinz* along with the *König*, *Markgraf* and *Grosser Kurfürst* out from the shelter of their base to support a squadron of destroyers going to the rescue of a U-boat, *U 20*, which had run aground off the Danish coast. The scale of the operation was unusual and resulted from the presence of one particular man marooned along with the crew in the U-boat. He was the U-boat commander, Kapitan Leutnant Walther Schwieger who had been responsible a year earlier for one of the Great War's most infamous events, the torpedoing of the Cunard liner *Lusitania* with the loss of 1,198 men, women and children. The destroyers had attempted to tow *U 20* off but she was so well entrenched in the sand that their hawsers snapped. All other efforts to free her failed and so the following morning her crew were taken off and she was blown up where she lay. At about 11 a.m. the battle group turned to head for home. At about 11.20 a.m. the group was spotted by the British submarine *J 1*, commanded by Commander Noel Laurence. At 12.08 p.m. he fired his first torpedo and successfully struck the *Grosser Kurfürst*. He fired again with the same deadly accuracy. The torpedo struck the *Kronprinz*, blasting a gaping hole in her side. Both stricken battleships began filling rapidly with water and yet were saved from sinking by their watertight compartments. They were able to limp back to the safe haven of their home port but had been put out of action for several months as a result of Commander Laurence's daring piece of seamanship. In a fitting reward for his actions and for surviving two hours of depth-charging by the German destroyers he was awarded a bar to his DSO.

During Fleet manoeuvres with the Third Battleship Squadron in the Heligoland Bight on 5 March 1917 the *Kronprinz* and *Grosser Kurfürst* collided at speed and both ships sustained considerable damage. The *Kronprinz* was speedily repaired and soon was in action again, part of a formidable force of ten battleships, one battle-cruiser, six cruisers and 50 torpedo-boat destroyers supporting the landing of 25,000 infantry on the Russian-held Baltic islands of Oesel, Dagoe and Moon in the Gulf of Riga. Apart from one more ill-fated naval venture against the British in April 1918, the *Kronprinz* would spend most of the rest of the war idle at her moorings.

By October 1918 the British blockade was strangling Germany and it had become clear that Germany was losing the war. A last-ditch battle plan was drawn up to try and inflict heavy losses on the British. German destroyers would raid shipping off the coast of Flanders and the Thames Estuary while the main German Battle Fleet gathered at the Schillig Roadstead anchorage. The destroyer action was designed to attract the attentions of the British Grand Fleet and lure it towards Terschelling, a Dutch island some 70 miles from the Ems River estuary. In this killing ground mines had already been sown and 25 U-boats lurked, ready to fall upon the unsuspecting British Fleet. Once the U-boats had weakened the British Fleet, the massive fire-power of the German High Seas Fleet would be brought to bear, crushing the British. At least, that was the plan. Word leaked out and spread like wildfire around the German Fleet, getting more and more exaggerated all the time. Soon it was rumoured that German Command had accepted a British challenge for a fight to the death; that the 69-year-old Admiral von Tirpitz had come out of retirement to take charge of the Fleet and lead it to its *Götterdämmerung*. It was even rumoured that the Kaiser would lead the Fleet into battle himself. The morale of the Fleet was low. They knew they had lost the war and were unwilling to risk their lives on a glorified but meaningless show of force.

The High Seas Fleet in line astern steams towards internment at Scapa Flow (Imperial War Museum)

The crews of the *Kronprinz, König* and *Markgraf* refused their orders to leave harbour. The mutiny spread and the plan was postponed as time and again the crews refused to put to sea. In frustration, on 31 October, German Command had *U 135* lay off the *Thüringen* and threaten a salvo from its torpedo tubes. Two loyal destroyers pulled alongside *Thüringen* and 200 marines went aboard to quell the rebellion. The mutineers fled to the fo'c'sle where they stood firm. Other mutineers on *Helgoland* trained their big guns on *U 135* and the destroyers and a dangerous stand-off developed. The crisis escalated when the loyal troops that had boarded *Thüringen* turned its guns on *Helgoland*. If someone started firing at such close range they would be very accurate and many deaths would result. The stand-off lasted for some time as everyone watched anxiously to see what would happen. Eventually the mutineers gave way and some 500 men from *Thüringen* and *Helgoland* were arrested.

The *Kronprinz* with the Third Squadron was sent to Kiel as the Fleet was dispersed. There mutiny flared again and this time as the mutiny grew it won the support of the townspeople. On 4 November the mutineers won control of Kiel and the *Kronprinz* was taken out to sea by loyal crew members to prevent her being seized by the communist revolutionaries and her mighty guns being turned against loyal strongholds ashore. The rebellion spread from town to town with red communist flags appearing everywhere. On 9 November the Kaiser abdicated and gave way to a communist régime. At five a.m. on Monday 11 November 1918 the Armistice was signed and hostilities ceased pending the peace negotiations.

As a condition of the Armistice the German High Seas Fleet would be taken into internment at Scapa Flow. Once the terms of internment had been resolved by the opposing forces the *Kronprinz* returned to port to

Aerial view of the High Seas Fleet in line astern

have her guns disarmed before she set off for internment at Scapa. She was soon boarded by uncontrollable mobs who systematically proceeded to loot the ship of everything they could get away with.

The entire British Grand Fleet rendezvoused with the High Seas Fleet in the North Sea to escort the former foe into internment at Scapa. Never had there been such a formidable gathering of naval fire-power at sea. Three hundred and seventy warships were brought together in close proximity with 90,000 men aboard. The British were taking no chances. They still suspected that the Germans were capable of a last-minute act of treachery. All British guns were loaded and trained on the High Seas Fleet, their crews at action stations. The British Grand Fleet formed up into two battle lines, six miles apart and stretching beyond sight into the distance. The High Seas Fleet then sailed through the passageway effectively created in single column towards internment at Scapa.

The High Seas Fleet arrived at Scapa over a period of days in late November 1918, the *Kronprinz* arriving on 27 November. There, the bulk of her crew of 1,136 were repatriated to Germany, leaving a skeleton crew of 200 to maintain her. Her guns had been disarmed before she left Germany for internment and so she was completely impotent.

At 10.30 a.m. on 21 June 1919, after some seven bleak months of internment, Admiral Ludwig von Reuter, in charge of the High Seas Fleet, scuttled the entire Fleet of some 74 warships to avoid it falling into the hands of the British. Disarmed, impotent, she was a shadow of her former self as her crew opened sea valves, smashed seawater pipes and condensers and prised out bulkhead rivets. Once the seacocks and valves were open their keys and handles were thrown overboard. They could never be closed again. The sea valves were disconnected from the upper deck to prevent any British marines who boarded her turning them off. Water flooded into the *Kronprinz* and she started to settle slowly into the sea. German sailors abandoned ship by lowering small boats over the side, thus alerting the British who sent a boarding party. Once aboard they found that they were unable to stop the flood of water into her. As the cold seawater rushing into her displaced air, her buoyancy became fatally altered. The weight of her superstructure and in particular her gun turrets (each of which weighed some 600 tons) eventually started bearing her over to one side. Two-and-three-quarter hours after the order to scuttle was given, at 1.15 p.m., the *Kronprinz* turned turtle and slipped beneath the waves of Scapa Flow and started her inverted descent through the black waters to the seabed 35 metres below.

The masts and superstructure of the *Kronprinz* hit the bottom first and now lie out at right angles on the seabed from the wreck. The colossal weight of the *Kronprinz* following on from above drove the superstructure deep into the soft seabed in an explosion of silt, causing the superstructure where the weight was greatest to crumple and distort. As the clouds of silt settled a fine layer of silt rained down on her upturned hull. The *Kronprinz* had made her final voyage. This would be her last resting place.

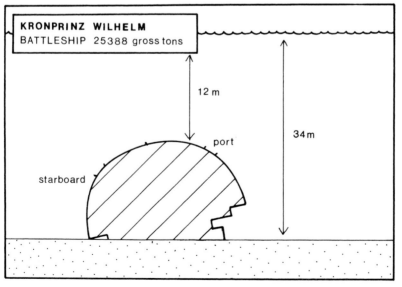

KRONPRINZ WILHELM
BATTLESHIP 25388 gross tons

12 m

34 m

port

starboard

The wreck of the
battleship *Kronprin
Wilhelm* with, in
the background, he
sister dreadnoughts
Markgraf and
König

Slowly over succeeding years she would sink deeper and deeper into the bottom of Scapa Flow.

The mighty German battleship *Kronprinz Wilhelm* today lies in 35 metres of water in the depths of Scapa Flow. She lies at Lat 58 53 39.0 N and Long 03 09 46.0 W out in the middle of the Flow and is one of the most exciting dives at Scapa. Her two sister dreadnoughts *König* and *Markgraf*, both weighing in at nearly 26,000 tons, lie on the seabed nearby. She lies upside-down with her starboard main deck resting on the seabed. After more than 70 years at the bottom of Scapa Flow she is now well settled into the soft silty seabed with much of her superstructure buried in the silt. To dive her you must drop down the now inverted side of her hull and find her main deck which runs off beneath the wreck into an awning chasm. The least depth over the whaleback of her upturned hull is 12 to 15 metres and she is best dived from one of the many dive-charter hard boats working the Flow.

At 575 feet in length she is so large and there is so much to see that there is little point in trying to return to the shot line to ascend. This would seriously eat into the amount of the wreck you can cover in any one dive. A number of dives are needed on the *Kronprinz* before you can become familiar with her and know your way about. The normal practice at Scapa, depending on the instructions of your particular dive marshal, is simply to ascend wherever you find yourself at the end of the dive. The skipper of the dive boat will be watching your bubble stream during the course of your dive and will know where you will be surfacing. If you are doing a decompression stop then it is a good idea to carry an inflatable marker which you can send up during your stop to ensure that the surface cover knows where you are.

The upturned keel of the *Kronprinz* is quite flat with only four one-metre-high bilge keels breaking its lines and designed to give a cutting edge to help the *Kronprinz* manoeuvre through the water. The hull slopes off towards the bow and stern. At the stern her three large propellers, easy prey for salvors, have been removed. The prop-shaft tunnels which once resounded to the thrash of the props themselves are now silent, dark, empty holes.

Salvors raised most of the scuttled High Seas Fleet during an epic salvage operation that spanned three decades from the 1920s to the 1940s. Although the *Kronprinz* largely escaped the attentions of those pioneering salvors she did not escape the attentions of other smaller-scale salvors who systematically worked her from then on to remove her valuable non-ferrous metals. As a result her hull shows a fair amount of damage around her engine-rooms, boiler rooms and torpedo rooms. At the stern, sections of the ship's bottom have been removed, revealing turbine blades, twisted boiler tubes and large dark voids built into the *Kronprinz* for safety. In the vicinity of the prop shafts her hull has been torn open like cardboard, revealing her double bottoms, shafts, gearing mechanisms and innards. On the whaleback of her upturned hull, about amidships, a large hole about 15 metres across has been blasted. This is a cavernous black void dropping down through several deck levels and allowing a fascinating insight into the *Kronprinz*. The structural stringers or ship's ribs are clearly visible inside. At the bow and stern there is more evidence of salvage blasting. The bow is heavily blasted and in places her hull loses its ship shape and begins to resemble a debris field. Here her hull has been ripped open and her valuable non-ferrous torpedo tubes salvaged. Divers have been known to spend a whole dive swimming around in this vast area, unable to orientate themselves and work out where they were.

As the dive boats manoeuvre into position over the wreck of the *Kronprinz* all eyes are on the bottom line on the dive boats' echo-sounders. For the last few minutes it has shown a relatively flat bottom at about 35 metres as the wreck site is approached. Suddenly the bottom line on the echo-sounder leaps straight up from 35 metres to 12 metres as the dive boat passes over the wreck. There is no mistaking such a huge trace on such a flat bottom. You have arrived over the wreck of the mighty *Kronprinz*. As the divers eagerly make last-minute checks on their own gear and do safety checks on their dive partners' gear the skipper throttles back and the dive boat slows to a stop right in position above the wreck. There is little current out here in the Flow to worry about and the wreck can be dived at all states of the tide. Like most of the German Fleet the *Kronprinz* is now usually buoyed and divers can follow the line down through the dark waters to the wreck far below. Finally the dive team is ready and one by one they leap from the safety of the dive boat to the water some eight feet below before congregating around the buoy.

As each dive team descends eyes strain down through the gloom for the first glimpse of the wreck below. Hearts race as the depth from the surface increases and the light filtering down fades. Below there is no sign of the wreck. The shot line seems to disappear straight down below into the darkness. As the descent continues the blackness below seems to take on a form. The silty seabed with its profusion of sponges and anemones seems to appear out of the gloom disappearing as far as the eye can see in either direction. As the divers land on the bottom it is only the unyielding feel of the normally soft silt and the regimented rows of rivets sticking up through it that discloses that this is the huge upturned hull of the *Kronprinz* that they have landed on. The divers then move off, finning towards the port side of the *Kronprinz* where the deck far below stands well clear of the seabed. On the starboard side the deck is well embedded in the silt and there is far less to see.

Normally the *Kronprinz* is buoyed just aft of midships on the more interesting port side. The divers fin over the upturned whaleback and reach the port side of the hull which plunges nearly vertically like a wall down to the main deck bulwark rail at a depth of approximately 30 metres, again well out of sight. The solid wall of the hull has many interesting features to take the divers' attention as they freefall down its side to the bulwark rail below. Rows of heavily encrusted portholes, some with the glass still in them, offer glimpses into the interior of the wreck. Halfway down the hull an open doorway, the door long gone, allows divers a better look inside. In port a gangway would have snaked up to here from the dock to allow access for crew and stores directly into the bowels of the ship.

As the divers drift down the side of the hull it becomes progressively darker. Although a lot of natural light illuminates the actual whaleback of the hull itself, down here the divers are in the shadow of the great hull and much of the natural light is blocked or filtered out before it can reach them. The divers' eyes soon go on to night vision, adjusting to the gloom. Although at first when they peered over the side of the hull they saw only blackness below, now they hardly notice any loss of visibility as they drift spellbound over the mighty wreck.

At a depth of 30 metres, the side of the hull that they have been following down stops abruptly and runs off at right angles under the wreck itself. The divers have reached the bulwark rail where the deck meets the side of the hull. Being upside-down the deck now leads the divers under the bulk of the wreck towards the superstructure embedded in the silt. From the bulwark rail down to the seabed easily visible below is a drop of five metres or so and effectively a huge black cavernous void has been created running along the majority of the port side of the hull. A torch is required to explore this yawning chasm properly and being upside-down, it can be difficult to recognise many of the features that are seen here at first glance.

Finning aft from the midships area the divers come across one of the *Kronprinz*'s secondary armaments; a 5.9-inch casemate rotating gun turret on the seabed, fallen from its mount above. Further aft another 5.9-inch casemate gun, still *in situ* in its turret points out defiantly from the side of the hull. On the seabed below there is a confused mass of torn hull plates and spars. Pushing far under the hull here it is possible to explore some of the upturned superstructure which surrounded the aftmost of the two mighty funnels. In places you can look down into open superstructure rooms that actually plunge beneath the level of the seabed for some distance. Everywhere large chunks of the famous coal that fired her boilers lie around. Some pieces of the coal have in the past been recovered and tried out in local open fires. Unfortunately the coal was found not suited for domestic fires as it was chosen specifically to be used in high-temperature furnaces.

Pressing further aft, the huge after superimposed 12-inch gun turret can be made out, its top buried in the seabed. These guns are some of the few main armament guns remaining today from any of the capital ships that fired at the Battle of Jutland in 1916. Their size is simply enormous. Set in the turret walls here and there are viewing slits designed to let the gun crews observe the effect of their actions. The huge twin 12-

inch barrels jut out from the turret pointing aft over (but now under) the aftmost 12-inch gun turret. The uppermost port side gun is clear of the seabed but the starboard side barrel is now lower and can be seen a few metres below, half covered in the silty seabed. Further aft can be found the aftmost 12-inch gun turret with both its 35-feet-long barrels clear of the seabed, their tips jammed into the teak deck planking above. Here and there are cable holders, their cables still neatly coiled around them. Some are still fixed to the upturned deck. Others have fallen from their rotted mounts to the seabed below. By now it is time for the divers to ascend. They will have glimpsed the sheer scale and majesty of the *Kronprinz* but have only explored a fraction of the ship. On other dives they will explore in the opposite direction moving forward along the wreck.

Moving forward from the midships mooring buoy along the casemate deck, more secondary armament 5.9-inch casemate rotating gun turrets are located, half recessed into the hull. Most of the single barrels are still *in situ* but pointing out or downwards at awkward angles. With the passage of time hull armour plating above has rotted away from its mounts and fallen to the seabed below, striking the protruding barrels of one or two of the guns. They quickly gave way to the tremendous weight of the armour plate and this has forced off the turret top of one of them.

Just aft of the bridge superstructure the four-foot-wide foremast can be seen lying flat on the seabed at 90 degrees to the hull. It is nearly intact and the cross rigging lies nearby. Finning along the mast away from the hull, the divers come across the mast's lower platform, the 5.9-inch gun control section. From here the fire from the secondary armament would be zeroed in on small vessels such as enemy destroyers attempting to attack with torpedoes at a battleship's most vulnerable aspect, its broadside. Further beyond lies the spotting top on its side. The top has fallen off it and inside it is now empty save for switches and hanging electric cables.

The seabed around the *Kronprinz* is littered with the debris that has resulted from the various salvage operations that have been mounted. Plates, pipes, broken pump casings and electric cables have created a debris field beside the wreck.

The *Kronprinz* makes for an exciting dive for many reasons. The sheer scale of the wreck means that it will take many dives to really get to know her. Each dive becomes something of a voyage of exploration. There is so much to see that even doing a repeat dive on the same area would reveal much that was missed on the first dive. The marine life around the *Kronprinz* is also good. The wreck itself has become an artificial reef covered with a rich carpet of marine life. Sponges, dead men's fingers, sea urchins and anemones all compete with each other for a foothold on this wreck. Schools of fish drift over the wreck and occasionally an inquisitive seal, perhaps from the colony on the nearby rocky haul-out site, the Barrel of Butter, will come in close to get a better look. Conger eels inhabit the deeper holes and recesses of the wreck, their steely, impassionate eyes watching the diver as he passes. As you drift over the wreck you are privileged to see one of the last remaining examples of the great dreadnoughts, a sight that non-divers cannot see. The dreadnought era has now passed into the history books and vanished from sight. All the once mighty dreadnoughts have, throughout the course of the century, been sunk or broken down for scrap. Most people can only read about this bygone age but for the diver here at Scapa Flow that era can still be experienced at first hand. The last guns to have been fired at the historic Battle of Jutland are there for you to gaze at, swim around and touch. Scapa Flow is an underwater museum, the *Kronprinz Wilhelm* one of the finest examples of man's ingenuity in his quest for supremacy of the seas.

Essential Information

Boat launch site: For RIBs, Houton Bay, Stromness Harbour, Scapa pier or Burray. Otherwise dive by hard boat.
Tidal conditions: $0-\frac{1}{2}$ knot maximum. Dive at any state of the tide.
Visibility: 10–20 metres average.
Maximum depth: Seabed 35 metres. Least depth over hull 12 metres.
Coastguard: Kirkwall (0856) 873268.
Police: Stromness (0856) 850222.
Recompression chamber: National Hyperbaric Centre Ltd, 123 Ashgrove Road West, Aberdeen (0224) 698895.
Air supplies: All the hard boats have onboard compressors.
Sea area: Fair Isle.
Hydrographic chart: No 35, Scapa Flow & Approaches.
Position: Lat 58 53 39.0 N, Long 03 09 46.0 W.

BIBLIOGRAPHY

Botting, Douglas and the Editors of Time-Life Books, *The U-boats*, Time-Life Books, Amsterdam, 1979.

British Sub Aqua Club (BSAC), *Wreck Registers for Scotland*, BSAC, 1987.

Brown, Malcolm and Patricia Meehan, *Scapa Flow*, Allen Lane, Penguin Press, 1968.

College, J. J., *Ships of the Royal Navy*.

Cousins, Geoffrey, *The Story of Scapa Flow*, Frederick Muller Ltd, 1965.

Cranna, J., *A Record of Shipwrecks in the Fraserburgh District*, Transactions of the Buchan Field Club, Peterhead, 1923.

Die Deutsche Flotte 1848–1945, Lohse-Eissing Verlag, Wilhemshaven, 1962.

Duckworth, Christian L. D. and Graham E. Langmuir, *Clyde and other Coastal Steamers*, T. Stephenson & Sons Ltd, Prescot, 1977.

Ferguson, David, *Shipwrecks of North-East Scotland 1444–1990*, Aberdeen University Press, 1991.

Ferguson, David, *Shipwrecks of Orkney, Shetland and Pentland Firth*, David & Charles, 1988.

Ferguson, David, *The Wrecks of Scapa Flow*, Orkney Press, 1985.

George, S. C., *Jutland to Junkyard*, Patrick Stephens, Cambridge, 1973.

Gosset, W. P., *Lost Ships of the Royal Navy*, London, 1986.

Groner, E., *Die Deutschen Kriegsschiffe 1815–1945*, Munich, 1966.

Hewison, William S., *This Great Harbour Scapa Flow*, Orkney Press, Kirkwall, 1985.

HMSO, *British Vessels Lost at Sea 1939–45*, Patrick Stephens, Cambridge, 1976.

Hocking, Charles F. L. A., *Dictionary of Disasters at Sea During the Age of Steam*, Lloyd's Register of Shipping, London, 1969.

Howarth, David and the Editors of Time-Life Books, *The Dreadnoughts*, Time-Life Books, Amsterdam, 1979.

Korganoff, Alexandre, *The Phantom of Scapa Flow*, Ian Allen, 1969.

Larn, R., *Shipwrecks of Britain and Ireland*.

Lloyd's War Losses–The Second World War, Volume I, London, 1989.

Lucas, W. E., *Eagle Fleet*, Weidenfeld and Nicolson, London, 1955.

Macdonald, Rod, *Dive Scapa Flow*, Mainstream, Edinburgh, 1990.

McDonald, Kendall, *Great British Wrecks*, Vol. 2, Underwater World Publications, London, 1986.

Marder, Arthur J., *From Dreadnought to Scapa Flow*, Oxford University Press, 1970.

Melrose, J., *Underwater Guide to the Clyde*.

Mitchell, W. H. & L. A. Sawyer, *British Standard Ships of World War I*, The Journal of Commerce and Shipping Telegraph Ltd, Liverpool, 1968.

Moir, Peter and Ian Crawford, *Clyde Shipwrecks*, Moir Crawford, Wemyss Bay, 1988.

Morris, Jeff, *The Story of the Fraserburgh Lifeboats*, Lifeboats Enthusiasts Society, Coventry, 1991.

Oban Divers Sub-Aqua Centre, *Underwater Guide*.

Reuter, Ludwig von, *Scapa Flow*, 1940.

Ridley Gordon, *Dive North-West Scotland*, Underwater World Publications, London, 1985.

Ridley, Gordon, *Dive West Scotland*, Underwater World Publications, London, 1984.

Ritchie, George F., *The Real Price of Fish, Aberdeen Steam Trawler Losses 1887–1961*, Hutton Press.

Rohwer, Jurgen, *Axis Submarine Successes 1939–45*, Patrick Stephens, Cambridge, 1983.

Rohwer, Jurgen, *Die U-Boot-ferfolge der Achsenmächte 1939–45*, J. F. Lehmanns Verlag, Munich, 1968.

Roskill, S. W., *The War At Sea, Vols I & II*, Collins, London, 1960.

Ruge, Vice-Admiral F., *Scapa Flow 1919*, Ian Allan, London, 1969.

Smith, Peter L., *The Naval Wrecks of Scapa Flow*, Orkney Press, 1989.

Taylor, J. C., *German Warships of World War I*, Ian Allan, London, 1971.

Taylor, J. C., *German Warships of World War II*, Ian Allan, London, 1966.

Young, John M., *Britain's Sea War, A Diary of Ship Losses 1939–45*, Wellingborough, 1989.

Vat, Dan van der, *The Grand Scuttle*, Hodder & Stoughton, London, 1982.

Zanelli, Leo, *Unknown Shipwrecks around Britain*, London, 1974.

Zanelli, Leo, *Shipwrecks Around Britain, A Diver's Guide*, Kaye & Ward, London, 1970.

Periodicals

Ayrshire Post
Daily Express
Diver Magazine
Dunoon Observer and *Argyllshire Standard*
Fraserburgh Herald

The Herald
Glasgow Evening News
Greenock Advertiser
Greenock Telegraph
Lloyds Register of Shipping
Lloyds Shipping Gazette and Weekly Summary
Lloyds Weekly Casualty Report
Oban Times
The Scotsman
Sea Breezes
Scottish Diver
Scottish Diving
Sport Diver
Sub Aqua Magazine
Sub Aqua Scene
Triton
Underwater World

INDEX